D1446831

A Primer for the Catechism of the Catholic Church

JOHN-PETER PHAM

A Primer for the
Catechism of the
Catholic Church

Foreword by
Most Reverend John J. Myers
Bishop of Peoria

MIDWEST THEOLOGICAL FORUM
Chicago, Illinois

This edition of
A Primer of the Catechism of the Catholic Church
is published by:

MIDWEST THEOLOGICAL FORUM
712 S. Loomis St.
Chicago, Illinois 60607
Tel. (312) 421-8135
Fax (312) 421-8129
e-mail: jsocias@msn.com

Second Edition 1997

Nihil Obstat: Rev. Msgr. Steven P. Rohlfs, S.T.D.
 Censor Librorum

Imprimatur: + Most Rev. John J. Myers, S.T.L., J.C.D.
 Bishop of Peoria

Cover illustration: taken from the Codex Christiani,
manuscript n. 3575 B. University of Bologna Library.
(courtesy of Tipografia Poliglotta Vaticana).

© John-Peter Pham 1994, 1997. All rights reserved.

ISBN 1-890177-01-6

Printed in the United States of America

Abbreviations

AA   Decree on the Apostolate of Lay People, *Apostolicam Actuositatem.*

CD   Decree on the Pastoral Office of Bishops in the Church, *Christus Dominus.*

CIC   Code of Canon Law, *Codex Iuris Canonici*

DS   Denzinger-Schönmetzer, *Enchiridion Symbolorum, definitionum et declarationum de rebus fidei et morum.*

DV   Dogmatic Constitution on Divine Revelation, *Dei Verbum.*

GS   Pastoral Constitution on the Church in the Modern World, *Gaudium et Spes.*

LG   Dogmatic Constitution on the Church, *Lumen Gentium.*

SC   Constitution on the Sacred Liturgy, *Sacrosanctum Concilium.*

Contents

Foreword

Each era in the long history of our Church has been characterized by its unique set of interconnected, and often inter-related, problems and opportunities. Situated in the midst of this complex is the catechetical mission of the Church, which strives to be faithful to the mystery of God's loving plan as it has been revealed in the life, death, and resurrection of Jesus Christ. This is communicated to us in the life of the Church, especially in her proclamation of the Word and celebration of the sacraments. While this catechetical mission is rooted in the handing on of the truths of our tradition, it must also strive to share these truths with the men and women of specific times and specific cultures in ways that relevantly address "in language intelligible to every generation, the ever recurring questions which men ask about the meaning of the present life and of the life to come, and how one is related to the other" (Gaudium et Spes, 4).

The Second Vatican Council was a major milestone in the history of our Church through which the Holy Spirit is leading members of the Church more deeply into the mystery of her faith and more surely into contact with the questions and concerns of the people of our own age. Through the Council, the Church is summoned by the voice of the Spirit to a genuine renewal so that "the nations might soon be led to the knowledge of truth and that the glory of God, which shines in the face of Jesus Christ, might shed its light on all men" (Ad Gentes, 42).

Consequently, our Holy Father, Pope John Paul II, understands the Catechism of the Catholic Church as one of the fruits of the conciliar renewal. Emerging as it does from the intense responses which the Council inspired in almost every aspect of the life of the Church, the Catechism clearly presents the faith and practice of the Church in continuity with her sacred tradition. "At the same time," according to the Holy Father, "the contents are often expressed in a 'new way' in order to respond to the questions of our age" (Fidei Depositum, 3).

A unifying thread running throughout the four main sections of the Catechism is the theme of the primacy of grace, the centrality of God's action in loving us even in our sins and saving us in Jesus Christ. Bishop Christoph von Schönborn, O.P., who had the major responsibility in the writing of the Catechism sees this "divine economy" as a theme of each of the document's sections: the economy of revelation which culminates in Jesus Christ becomes a sacramental economy in the life of the Church which serves the "dispensation of the mystery." This economy calls for a unique Way of Life, assisted by the power of grace, on the part of the disciple of Christ as well as the prayerful response of each human heart. (Cf.

James Socias, ed., Reflections on the Catechism of the Catholic Church, *Chicago: Midwest Theological Forum, 1993, pp. 78-79)*

The Holy Father has addressed the Catechism not only to the bishops and clergy, who share in a special way in the catechetical mission of the Church, but also to the entire People of God. As the Catechism is written, it is truly accessible to many people who will find in it a clear exposition of the faith and practice of the Church. It is to be "a sure and authentic reference for the teaching of Catholic doctrine and particularly for preparing local catechisms" (Fidei Depositum, 4). In fact, Archbishop Crescenzio Sepe, secretary of the Congregation of Clergy, which has responsibility for catechesis, noted that it is a "model and exemplar," which is a sure norm for our faith and a great aid in the preparation of our own catechetical materials. (cf. Socias, Reflections . . . , *p. 235)*

Father John-Peter Pham, a priest of the Diocese of Peoria, has prepared this volume which is based clearly on the Catechism of the Catholic Church. His skills at exposition, already evident in a significant array of publications, are brought here to bear in a synthetic way to produce a question and answer introduction to the Catechism. Both the questions and the answers, while rooted in the perennial proclamation of the Church—as witnessed by the many quotations from magisterial documents—are also sensitive to the contemporary concerns of both believers and of those who are searching for faith. His work is faithful to the structure of the Catechism as well as to its content. Those who read this Primer for the Catechism of the Catholic Church *will be exposed to some of the basic concepts and categories of our Catholic faith and practice and their interconnection. Anything retained in memory will become a point of reference in the various situations in which we all find ourselves, allowing the Gospel, as it has been entrusted to the Church, to exercise its power in our lives. I do not hesitate to recommend this* Primer *to anyone who wishes assistance in beginning to use the Catechism of the Catholic Church or who, for whatever reason, prefers a more succinct reference work.*

May Mary, Mother of God and Mother of the Church, intercede for rich blessings on all who seek the renewal of the Church through catechetics and, in a special way, for those who seek this end through the use of this Primer.

+ Most Reverend John J. Myers
Bishop of Peoria

Preface to the First Edition

"Guarding the deposit of faith is the mission which the Lord has entrusted to his Church and which she fulfills in every age." With these words Pope John Paul II opens the Apostolic Constitution Fidei Depositum, *which promulgated the long awaited* Catechism of the Catholic Church. *The great importance of catechesis in the transmission of this faith can be seen from the very beginning in the commission which was given to the Apostles by the Risen Lord: "Go therefore and make disciples of all nations, baptizing them in the name of the Father and of the Son and of the Holy Spirit, teaching them to observe all that I have commanded you" (Mt. 28:19-20). Recognition of this mission is reflected in the lofty goals which the Holy Father set for catechetical instruction, noting that it should . . . faithfully and systematically present the teaching of Sacred Scripture, the living Tradition of the Church and the authentic Magisterium of the Church, as well as the spiritual heritage of the Fathers and of the Church's saints, to allow for a better knowledge of the Christian mystery and for enlivening the faith of the People of God. It should take into account the doctrinal statements which down the centuries the Holy Spirit has instituted to his Church. It should also help illumine with the light of faith the new situations and problems which had not yet emerged in the past. (Fidei Depositum, 3) In this context, the Holy Father presented the* Catechism of the Catholic Church *to the People of God as a "sure norm for teaching the faith"* (Fidei Depositum, 4) *and, along with the Code of Canon Law, the final touch on the program of the Second Vatican Council.*

Despite this recommendation, many nevertheless will find the Catechism *an imposing text with its more than seven hundred pages, filled with over 3,600 citations from Scripture, the Fathers, and Magisterial documents. It is to these members of the People of God that this* Primer for the Catechism of the Catholic Church *is addressed. Using the* Catechism *itself, along with other documents, as references, this book seeks to provide a question-and-answer summary of the contents of the original. While this* Primer *is no substitute for the* Catechism of the Catholic Church, *it is hoped that it may nonetheless whet the appetites of its readers for the original as well as serve as a useful companion for their study of the Church's new "sure and authentic reference text for teaching Catholic doctrine"* (Fidei Depositum, 4). *And if this simple manner of presentation may seem to some to be somewhat simplified, I beg pardon in the words of St. Cyril of Jerusalem, author of one of the Church's earliest catechisms: "I think it is well at this time to present a short compendium of the necessary doctrines . . . let those present who are of more mature understanding be patient as they listen to an introductory course suited to children, milk for sucklings. In this way, those who need catechetical instruction will profit and those who have the knowledge will revive the memory that they already know."*

I should like to express my profound thanks to my superiors and colleagues both in Rome and in Peoria for their encouragement and assistance with this book, among many other undertakings. In particular, I want to thank His Excellency, the Most Reverend John Joseph Myers, Bishop of Peoria, for his constant support as well as for his kind foreword; the Reverend Richard Soseman for his suggestions and help in proof-reading.

Finally, with deep gratitude and affection, I dedicate this work to my parents, who raised me in the faith and - in their own roundabout way - nurtured my priestly vocation, and to His Excellency, the Most Reverend François-Xavier Nguyen van Thuan, Titular Archbishop of Vadesi, who helped me to keep that faith and brought that vocation to fruition and whose generous support made the publication of this book possible.

John-Peter Pham
Rome, Solemnity of the Body and Blood of Christ, 1994

Preface to the Second Edition

The publication of this second, revised edition of A Primer for the Catechism of the Catholic Church *gives me the happy opportunity to thank the many people who have made it possible. I renew my thanks to those individuals already mentioned in the preface to the first edition. If anything, the intervening three years have revealed to me all the more clearly the debt of gratitude which I owe to each one of them.*

To this list, I would want to add the names of all those who have responded to the Primer *by writing me with their suggestions and criticisms. Their helpfulness has contributed much more to this edition.*

Thanks are also in order to the Rev. James Socias and the staff of the Midwest Theological Forum for their support and encouragement.

Finally, I want to thank the Very Rev. Terrance P. O'Brien and the parish community of St. Matthew's Catholic Church, Champaign, Illinois, for a most congenial home wherein these pages were revised. It is, first and foremost, for the building up of the Bride of Christ, the Church, in each of her members at the most basic level, that this little book is being made available again. With God's grace, may it indeed be ad utilitatem quoque nostram totiusque Ecclesiae suae sanctae.

John-Peter Pham
Champaign, Illinois,
Feast of the Exaltation of the Holy Cross, 1997

Part One:
The Profession of Faith

Section I:

"I Believe, We Believe"

1. What is our deepest desire?

27*

We are created with a profound desire for God since it is "in Him we live and move and have our being" (Acts 17:28).

2. How is this desire expressed?

28

The desire for God is expressed in man's continual pursuit throughout history for the ultimate truth and goodness, as seen by various prayers and rituals in every culture.

3. How do we come to a knowledge of God?

31-35

We can come to a natural knowledge of God through the material world—which presents evidence of its Creator through its contingency, order and beauty—and through the very stirrings of our hearts which aspire to God: "You have made us for yourself and our hearts find no peace until they rest in you" (St. Augustine, *Confessions* I,1).

4. What is the content of this natural knowledge of God?

36-38

This natural knowledge of God consists in the fact that "those things, which in themselves are not beyond the grasp of human reason, can, in the present condition of the human race, be known by all men with ease, with firm certainty, and without the contamination of error" (DV 6).

---

* The numerical references on the margins of the page refer to the appropriate paragraphs of the *Catechism of the Catholic Church*.

39-43   **5. On the basis of this natural knowledge, what can we say about God?**

While the infinite perfections of God are beyond the limited scope of our human imagination and language, we can nonetheless speak of God since "from the greatness and the beauty of created things, their original author, by analogy, is seen" (Wis. 13:5).

51-52   **6. How do we come to know about the mystery of God himself?**

We come to know of the mystery of God himself only because, in his love, he reveals himself to us.

53   **7. How does God reveal himself to us?**

God reveals himself to us through deeds and words "which are intrinsically bound up with each other. As a result, the works performed by God in the history of salvation show forth and bear out the doctrine and the realities signified by the words; the words, for their part, proclaim the works, and bring to light the mystery they contain" (DV 2).

54-64   **8. How has God revealed himself in the course of human history?**

God "manifested himself to our first parents from the very beginning. After the fall, he buoyed them up with the hope of salvation, by promising redemption. . . . In his own time God called Abraham, and made him a great nation. After the era of the patriarchs, he taught this nation, by Moses and the prophets, to recognize him as the only living and true God. . . . He taught them, too, to look for the promised Savior" (DV 3).

65-74   **9. What is the culmination of this history of revelation?**

After "God spoke in fragmentary and varied ways to our fathers through the prophets, in this, the final age, he has spoken to us through his Son" (Heb. 1:1-2). In Jesus Christ, God has made his definitive revelation of himself to humanity. God "wants all men to be saved and come to know the truth" (1 Tim. 2:4), that is, to know Jesus Christ.

10. How was this saving truth handed down? 75-79

This saving truth, which is the Gospel, was entrusted by Jesus Christ to his disciples and is handed down to us through their oral preaching, which formed Tradition, and their writings, which formed the New Testament of the Bible.

11. What is the relationship between Tradition and Scripture? 80-83

Tradition and Scripture "make up a single sacred deposit of the Word of God, which is entrusted to the Church" (DV 10).

12. How are these two parts of the one Word of God to be interpreted? 84-90

The task of interpreting the Word of God, whether received through Tradition or Scripture, is "entrusted to the living teaching office of the Church alone. Its authority in this matter is exercised in the name of Jesus Christ" (DV 10).

13. How is knowledge of this deposit of faith increased? 91-95

The faithful grow in knowledge of this deposit of faith through contemplation and study of the sacred sciences and the interior meditation on the Word of God as well as through the teaching of those who, through apostolic succession, have a particular charism to transmit this Word.

101-
104
14. How does God communicate himself to us through the Bible?

In his marvelous condescension, God speaks to us in human words: "Indeed the words of God, expressed in the words of men, are in every way like human language, just as the Word of the eternal Father, when he took on himself the flesh of human weakness, became like men" (DV 13).

105-
108
15. What does the Church mean when she professes that the Bible is inspired?

When the Church professes her faith in the inspiration of Scripture, it means that in the writing of the sacred books, "God chose certain men who, all the while he employed them in this task, made full use of their powers and faculties so that, though he acted in them and by them, it was as true authors that they consigned to writing whatever he wanted written, and no more" (DV 11).

109-
114
16. How are we to read and interpret sacred Scripture?

We should read and interpret sacred Scripture with its divine authorship in mind. Concretely, this means that we must pay close attention to the contents and unity of the entire Scripture, the living Tradition of the Church, and the "analogy of faith," the interrelationship of the truths of faith within the entirety of revelation.

115-
119
17. What are the senses of Scripture?

According to ancient tradition, two senses or meanings can be found in Scripture. The *literal sense* refers to what is meant by the actual words of Scripture as uncovered by careful study of the text. The *spiritual sense* refers to the symbolic meanings which can be found in the words, events, and objects mentioned in Scripture.

18. What is the "Canon" of Scripture?   120

The "Canon" of Scripture is the list of those books which Tradition has discerned as inspired by God and, consequently, form the two Testaments of the Bible.

19. How many books make up the Canon of the Old Testament?

Forty-six books form the Canon of the Old Testament according to the constant teaching of the Church: Genesis, Exodus, Leviticus, Numbers, Deuteronomy, Joshua, Judges, Ruth, 1 and 2 Samuel, 1 and 2 Kings, 1 and 2 Chronicles, Ezra, Nehemiah, Tobit, Judith, Esther, 1 and 2 Maccabees, Job, Psalms, Proverbs, Ecclesiastes, Song of Songs, Wisdom, Sirach, Isaiah, Jeremiah, Lamentations, Baruch, Ezekiel, Daniel, Hosea, Joel, Amos, Obadiah, Jonah, Micah, Nahum, Habakkuk, Zephaniah, Haggai, Zechariah, and Malachi.

20. How many books make up the Canon of the New Testament?

Twenty-seven books form the Canon of the New Testament according to the constant teaching of the Church: Matthew, Mark, Luke, John, Acts of the Apostles, Romans, 1 and 2 Corinthians, Galatians, Ephesians, Philippians, Colossians, 1 and 2 Thessalonians, 1 and 2 Timothy, Titus, Philemon, Hebrews, James, 1 and 2 Peter, 1, 2, and 3 John, Jude, and Revelation.

21. What is the relationship between the two Testaments?   121-
130

Since apostolic times, the Church has taught that both Testaments exist in a unity based upon the divine will: "God, the inspirer and author of the books of both Testaments, in his wisdom has so brought it about that the New should be hidden in the Old and that the Old should be made manifest in the New. For, although Christ founded the New Covenant in his blood, still the books of the Old Testament, all of them caught up into the Gospel message, attain and show forth their full meaning in the New Testament and, in their turn, shed light on it and explain it" (DV 16).

131-133

22. What is the role of Scripture in the life of the Church?

The sacred Scripture enjoys a preeminent place in the life of the Church, which "has always venerated the divine Scriptures as she venerated the Body of the Lord, in so far as she never ceases, particularly in the sacred liturgy to partake of the bread of life and offer it to the faithful from the one table of the Word of God and the Body of Christ. She has always regarded, and continues to regard the Scriptures, taken together with sacred Tradition, as the supreme rule of her faith. For, since they are inspired by God and committed to writing once and for all time, they present God's own Word in an unalterable form, and they make the voice of the Holy Spirit sound again and again" (DV 21).

144-149

23. What is the "obedience of faith"?

"Obedience of faith" means to freely submit oneself to the Word which is received, because its truth is guaranteed by God, who is Truth itself. Abraham is a model of this obedience, while the Virgin Mary is its realization *par excellence*.

24. What is faith?

Faith is the personal adhesion of man in his entirety to God who has revealed himself. This includes an adhesion of the intellect and the will to the revelation which God has made of himself by his actions and words. The act of believing itself has reference to both the truth which is believed and to the person who attests to its truth value. The Christian, therefore, can be said to believe in, as well as because, of the one God, Father, Son, and Holy Spirit.

25. What is the relationship between personal faith and the faith of the Church? 150-165

Although the act of faith is the personal response of an individual to the God's revelation, it can never be an isolated act. Each believer receives his faith through the Church, which precedes, germinates, and nourishes this faith. As the Tradition of the Church expresses this in the well-known proverb, "He cannot have God for his Father who does not have the Church for his Mother" (St. Cyprian, *The Unity of the Church* 5).

Section II:

The Christian Profession of Faith

26. Who is the God we believe in?

199-237

"We believe and confess. . . . That there is one highest, incomprehensible and ineffable reality, which is truly Father, Son, and Holy Spirit; the three persons together, and each person distinctly; therefore in God there is only Trinity . . . because each of the persons in that reality, that divine substance, essence or nature which alone is the beginning of all things, apart from which nothing else can be found. This reality is neither generating nor generated, nor proceeding, but it is the Father who generates, the Son who is generated and the Holy Spirit who proceeds, so that there be distinctions between the persons but unity in nature" (Lateran Council IV, *On the Errors of Abbot Joachim*: DS 804). This one God reveals himself to us as Truth and Love.

27. How do we come to a knowledge of God as Trinity?

238-260

We arrive at the knowledge of God as Trinity only through the self-revelation of God. Through his Incarnation, the Son of God revealed God to be the eternal Father with whom he is consubstantial. The mission in time of the Spirit, sent by the Father through the Son, likewise reveals the third person of the Trinity as part of the one Godhead.

28. How does God reveal himself as "almighty"?

268-274

God reveals his omnipotence in converting us from our sins and restoring us to his friendship through grace.

As the Church recalls in the Liturgy, "Father, you show your almighty power in your mercy and forgiveness. . . . " (Roman Missal, Collect for the 26th Sunday in Ordinary Time).

279-
314

29. Who created the universe?

God alone created—that is, brought into being out of nothing—the entire universe. He did so freely and directly, without any assistance or pre-existent matter or substance. God continues to maintain the universe in its existence through his Son, who is "the reflection of the Father's glory, the exact representation of the Father's being, and he sustains all things by his powerful Word" (Heb. 1:3).

30. Why did God create the universe?

God created the universe to manifest and communicate his glory. That his creatures would share in his truth, goodness, and beauty, in turn, gives glory to God.

325-
349

31. What are angels?

Angels are spiritual creatures of God, created to glorify him without ceasing and to serve his salvific plan towards the rest of creation.

355-
379

32. Who created man?

"God created man in his image; in the divine image he created him, male and female he created them" (Gen. 1:27). God created him as both material and spiritual being and established him in the divine friendship: "You formed man in your own likeness and set him over the whole world to serve you, his creator, and to rule over all creatures" (Roman Missal, Eucharistic Prayer IV).

33. What is sin?

385-390

Sin is an abuse of freedom in an act of disobedience to God which manifests a lack of confidence in his infinite goodness. As a consequence of sin, the profound relationship of friendship and communion between God and man is broken.

34. When did sin enter the world?

391-412

"Although set by God in a state of rectitude, man, enticed by the evil one, abused his freedom at the very start of history" (GS 13). This, of course, presupposes an earlier act of rebellion against God by certain angels.

35. What is this sin called?

This sin is called original sin because through it "sin entered the world and with sin, death" (Rom. 5:12).

36. What are the effects of original sin?

By their sin, the original parents lost their original state of holiness and justice which they had received from God, not only for themselves, but for all humanity. To their descendants, therefore, they transmitted a human nature wounded by their original sin and, consequently, deprived of the original condition of holiness and justice.

37. Who is Jesus?

422-429

From the perspective of human history, Jesus of Nazareth was a Jew, being born in Bethlehem of Judea to a daughter of Israel, during the time of Herod the Great and the sovereignty of Caesar Augustus. By profession a carpenter, he was crucified and died at Jerusalem under the procuratorship of Pontius Pilate. However, from the perspective of our Christian faith, we can add that we "believe in Our Lord Jesus Christ, the Son of God. He is the eternal Word, born of the Father before all ages, and one in substance with the Father, through whom all things were made. He was incarnate of the Holy Spirit, from the Virgin Mary, and was made man. . . . He dwelt among us full of grace and of truth. He proclaimed and established the Kingdom of God, manifesting the Father to us in Himself. He gave us His new commandment that we are to love one another as He loved us. He taught us the way of the evangelical Beatitudes. . . . He died for us, affixed to a Cross, bringing salvation to us by the blood of redemption. He was buried, arose by his own power. . . . He ascended into Heaven, whence he will come again, this time in glory, to judge the living and the dead" (Paul VI, *Credo of the People of God* 12).

430-
435

38. What does the name "Jesus" mean?

In Hebrew, the name "Jesus" means "God who saves." Thus, the child born of the Virgin Mary was called "Jesus" because "he will save his people from their sins" (Mt. 1:21).

436-
440

39. What does "Christ" mean?

The title "Christ" in the Greek of the New Testament means "anointed" and has its origins in the Hebrew term "Messiah." Jesus is the Christ because "God anointed him with the Holy Spirit and power" (Acts 10:38).

441-
445

40. What does it mean that Jesus Christ is the "Son of God"?

The title "Son of God" refers to the unique and eternal relationship between Jesus Christ and God his Father. He is "the only Son coming from the Father" (Jn. 1:14) and is the eternal Word who "was in God's presence . . . and was God" (Jn. 1:1). The belief in Jesus Christ as the Son of God is an absolutely necessary condition for being a Christian since "anyone who denies the Son has no claim on the Father" (1 Jn. 2:23).

41. What does it mean that Jesus Christ is "Lord"?

446-451

The title of "Lord" refers to the divine sovereignty. There-fore, to profess that Jesus Christ is "Lord" is to believe in his divinity.

42. What is the Incarnation?

456-478

In the fullness of time, the only Son of the Father, the eternal Word consubstantial with the Father, became incarnate, that is, without losing his divine nature, he assumed a human nature and was born of the Virgin Mary. Jesus Christ thus possesses two natures, divine and human, without mixing them, but rather uniting them in the person of the Son of God.

43. Why did the Incarnation take place?

Through the Incarnation, Jesus Christ is true God and true man, united in one divine person. For this reason, he is capable of being the only mediator between God and man who could restore the communion between God and man lost in the original sin.

44. What is the Immaculate Conception?

484-494

Because of the "predestination of the Blessed Virgin as Mother of God" (LG 61), she was "from the first mo-ment of her conception, by a singular grace and privi-lege of almighty God, in view of the merits of Christ Jesus the Savior of the human race, preserved free from all stain of original sin" (Pius IX, *Ineffabilis Deus* 39: DS 2803).

45. Why is the Virgin Mary called "Mother of God"?

495-507

Mary is called "Mother of God" because she is the mother of the eternal Son of God who was made man, that is to say, God himself.

595-
618
46. What is the significance of the sufferings of Jesus Christ?

In delivering up his Son for our sins, God revealed his plan for us as a loving design which exceeds any merit on our part: "Love, then, consists in this: not that we have loved God, but that he has loved us and has sent his Son as an offering for our sins" (1 Jn. 4:10). Because of the universal salvific will of God—"it is no part of your heavenly Father's plan that a single one of these little ones shall ever come to grief" (Mt. 18:14)—Jesus Christ came "not to be served, but to serve, to give his own life as a ransom for many" (Mt. 20:28).

47. What is the significance of the death of Jesus Christ?

The death of Jesus Christ is simultaneously the *paschal sacrifice* of "the Lamb who takes away the sins of the world" (Jn. 1:29) and brings about the definitive re-demption of man and the *sacrifice of the New Covenant* which restores man to communion with God. This sac-rifice is unique and unsurpassable because it is the offering of God himself, the Son, to God himself, the Father, through God himself, the Holy Spirit.

631-
635
48. What do we mean when we say that Jesus "descended into hell"?

When we use the expression "descended into hell" in reference to Jesus, we mean that Jesus was truly dead and that by his death for us, he conquered death and the devil, the "prince of death" (Heb. 2:14). In death, Christ, his soul united with his divine person, descended into the realm of the dead to open the way to heaven for those just who had died previous to his redemptive sacrifice on the cross.

638-
650
49. What was the resurrection of Jesus Christ?

While we are unable to completely fathom the mysteries of God's greatest work, we can assert that the resurrection of Jesus Christ was essentially different from any of the resurrections of the dead which he himself worked before Easter. These resurrected persons—the daughter of Jairus, the son of the widow of Naim, and Lazarus—died once again in time. In contrast, in his resurrected body, Jesus Christ passed beyond time and space. The body of Jesus, in the resurrection, was filled with the power of the Holy Spirit and now participates in the divine life in a state of glory.

50. What is the significance of the resurrection of Jesus Christ? 651-655

The resurrection of Jesus Christ, above all, constitutes the confirmation of all he did and taught: "And if Christ had not been raised, our preaching is void of content, and your faith is empty too" (1 Cor. 15:14). Thus, the promises made to Abraham and his descendants in the Old Testament are fulfilled and the truth of the divinity of Christ affirmed. Likewise, the resurrection of Jesus Christ is the basis for our own future resurrection: "Christ is now raised from the dead, the first fruits of those who have fallen asleep. Death came through a man; hence the resurrection of the dead through a man also. Just as in Adam all die, so in Christ all will come to life again" (1 Cor. 15:20-22).

51. What does it mean that Jesus Christ "ascended into heaven and is seated at the right hand of the Father"? 659-664

The ascension of Jesus Christ marks the definitive entry of the humanity of Jesus into the heavenly realm of God, from where he will come again. As Jesus Christ, the Head of the Church, has preceded us into the Kingdom of the Father, so we too have hope that one day we will be reunited there with him for all eternity.

668-
679

52. What does it mean that Christ "will come again to judge the living and the dead"?

When the Church professes her faith that Jesus Christ "will come again to judge the living and the dead," she means that at the end of time, on the Day of Judgment, her Lord will come in glory to effect the definitive triumph of good over evil. At this coming, Christ will reveal the secret dispositions of every heart and judge "each according to his own merits: those who will have responded to the Love and Mercy of God will go into life eternal, but those who will have rejected them, right to the end, will be given over to the fire that will never cease. And there will be no end to His kingdom" (Paul VI, *Credo of the People of God* 12).

683-
741

53. What does the Church profess about the Holy Spirit?

The Church professes her belief in "the Holy Spirit, the Lord and the One who gives life, who is adored and glorified together with the Father and the Son. He spoke through the Prophets; He was sent to us by Christ after his Resurrection and Ascension to the Father; He illuminates, vivifies, watches over and guides the Church, and purifies her members so long as they do not resist Grace. His action, which reaches to the depths of the soul, makes man capable of responding to that precept of Christ: Be perfect as your heavenly Father is perfect" (Paul VI, *Credo of the People of God* 13).

748-
776

54. What is the Church?

The Church is the assembly of those who are called by the Word of God to form the People of God and who, nourished by the Body of Christ, become themselves the Body of Christ. Prefigured in creation, prepared by the old Covenant, founded by the words and actions of Jesus Christ—most of all through his cross and resurrection—the Church is revealed in the mystery of salvation through the effusion of Holy Spirit on Pentecost. In a mystery which only faith can comprehend, the Church has both a visible and a spiritual dimension: she is simultaneously a hierarchical society and the mystical Body of Christ. The Church, "in Christ, is likened to a sacrament: a sign and instrument, that is, of communion with God and of unity among all men" (LG 1).

55. What are the properties of the Church? 811

The properties of the Church are that she is one, holy, catholic, and apostolic.

56. What does it mean that the Church is "one"? 813-822

The Church is "one" because her members share in "one Lord, one faith, one baptism, one God and Father of all" (Eph. 4:5-6).

57. What does it mean that the Church is "holy"? 823-831

The Church is "holy" because of the work of the Trinity: the Father most holy is her origin and Lord, Christ is her spouse and gave himself over to sanctify her, and the Holy Spirit gives life to her. Although the individual members of the Church may be sinners, the Church itself remains the stainless bride of Christ.

58. What does it mean that the Church is "catholic"? 832-856

The Church is "catholic" ("universal") because she alone proclaims the totality of truth, she alone administers the fullness of the means of salvation, she alone is sent to all peoples and addresses herself to all men, and she alone embraces all times and places.

59. What does it mean that the Church is "apostolic"? 857-865

The Church is "apostolic" because she is built on the foundation of the "twelve apostles of the Lamb" (Rev.

21:14), indestructible, and infallibly maintained in the truth. Christ governs her through the ministry of Peter and the apostles and through their successors, the Pope and the College of Bishops.

871-879

60. Why are there distinctions between the different ministries and offices in the Church?

There are different ministries in the Church because "in order to shepherd the People of God and to increase its numbers without cease, Christ the Lord set up in his Church a variety of offices which aim at the good of the whole body. The holders of office, who are invested with a sacred power, are, in fact, dedicated to promoting the interests of their brethren, so that all who belong to the people of God, and are consequently endowed with true Christian dignity, may, through their free and well-ordered efforts towards a common goal, attain to salvation" (LG 18).

880-896

61. What is the hierarchy of the Church?

Christ, in instituting the Twelve, "constituted them in the form of a college or permanent assembly, at the head of which he placed Peter, chosen from amongst them" (LG 19) and "so in like fashion, the Roman Pontiff, Peter's successor, and the bishops, the successors of the apostles" (LG 22).

62. What is the universal power of the Pope?

Jesus Christ chose Simon, to whom he gave the name of Peter, to be the visible foundation of his Church. The Pope, as Bishop of Rome, is successor of Peter and thus is "the head of the College of Bishops, Vicar of Christ and Pastor of the universal Church on earth" (CIC, c. 331). As such, the Pope "has been granted by God supreme, full, immediate and universal power in the care of souls. As pastor of all the faithful his mission is to promote the common good of the universal Church and the particular good of all the churches. He is therefore endowed with the primacy of ordinary power over all the Churches" (CD 2).

63. What is the infallibility of the Pope?

The infallibility of the Pope means that he, when "acting in the office of shepherd and teacher of all Christians, he defines, by virtue of his supreme apostolic authority, a doctrine concerning faith or morals to be held by the universal Church, possesses through the divine assistance promised to him in the person of Blessed Peter, the infallibility with which the divine Redeemer willed His Church to be endowed" (Vatican Council I, *Pastor Aeternus*: DS 3074).

64. What is meant by the term "laity"?

897-913

The "laity" is "understood to mean all the faithful except those in Holy Orders and those who belong to a religious state approved by the Church" (LG 31). "The characteristic of the lay state being a life led in the midst of the world and of secular affairs, lay people are called by God to make of their apostolate, through the vigor of their Christian spirit, a leaven in the world" (AA 2).

65. What is "consecrated life"?

914-933

The term "consecrated life" characterizes those members of the faithful who, by public profession of the evangelic counsels of poverty, chastity, and obedience, live in an established (and usually, although not necessarily, communal) state of life recognized by the Church.

66. What does the term "communion of saints" mean?

946-959

The term "communion of saints" refers, first of all, to the "holy things," preeminent among which is the sacrament of the Eucharist, through which "the unity of believers, who form one body in Christ, is both expressed and brought about. The term also refers to the Church's belief that the "communion of all Christ's faithful, those who are pilgrims on earth, those who have died and are being purified, and those who are enjoying heavenly beatitude, all coalesce into one Church; and likewise we believe that in this communion there is at hand for us the merciful love of God and of his Saints, who also lend favorable ears to our prayers" (Paul VI, *Credo of the People of God* 30).

963-
972
67. What is the role of the Virgin Mary in this communion of saints?

"The Most Blessed Virgin Mary Immaculate, conjoined by a close and indissoluble bond to the mystery of the Incarnation and Redemption, having completed the course of her earthly life, was assumed body and soul to heavenly glory, and, rendered like unto her Son Who rose from the dead, received the lot of the just antecedently: We believe that the Most Holy Mother of God, the new Eve, Mother of the Church, continues now in Heaven to perform her maternal function with respect to the members of Christ, by which she contributes to the engendering and growth of divine life in each of the souls of redeemed men" (Paul VI, *Credo of the People of God* 15).

988-
1014
68. What is meant by the "resurrection of the dead"?

In death, the soul is separated from the body. However, just as Christ died and rose to live forever, so likewise on the last day, our bodies will be raised, transformed, and united with our souls.

1020-
1050
69. What do we mean when we profess our belief in "life everlasting"?

When we profess our belief in "life everlasting," we acknowledge that "We believe in eternal life. We believe that the souls of all those who have died in the Grace of Christ—whether those who must yet be purified in the fire of Purgatory, or those who at once, and separated from their bodies, like the Good Thief, are received by Jesus into Paradise—constitute the People of God after death, which will be done with on the day of resurrection, when these souls will be united with their bodies. We believe that the multitude of those souls gathered together with Jesus and Mary in Paradise constitutes the Church of Heaven, where these same souls, enjoying eternal beatitude, see God as He is, and also, certainly in diverse degree and manner, have a share with the holy angels in the divine governance of things which the glorified Christ exercises. . . . Professing this faith and buoyed by this hope, we long for the resurrection of the dead and the life of the world to come" (Paul VI, *Credo of the People of God* 28-30).

Part Two:
The Celebration of the
Christian Mystery

Section I:

The Sacramental Economy

70. What is the liturgy?

The word "liturgy" is derived from the Greek term 1066-
leitourgia, meaning "work of the people," which was 1109
used to refer to any public duty or service. In theological usage, the term refers to the official public worship
of the Church, as distinguished from private devotion.
Nevertheless, the liturgy is more than this since "Christ,
indeed, always associates the Church with himself in
this great work in which God is perfectly glorified and
men are sanctified. The Church is his beloved Bride
who calls to her Lord, and through him offers worship
to the eternal Father. The liturgy, then, is rightly seen
as an exercise of the priestly office of Jesus Christ. It
involves the presentation of man's sanctification under the guise of the signs perceptible by the senses and
its accomplishment in ways appropriate to each of these
signs" (SC 7).

71. What is a sacrament?

1131-
A sacrament is an efficacious sign of grace, instituted 1130
by Christ and entrusted to the Church, which transmits
to us the divine life through its employ. The Church
recognizes seven sacraments: baptism, confirmation,
the Eucharist, reconciliation, anointing of the sick,
marriage, and holy orders. The visible rites with which
the sacraments are celebrated both express and realize
the graces proper to each sacrament.

72. What is the purpose of the sacraments?

"The purpose of the sacraments is to sanctify men, to build up the Body of Christ, and, finally, to give worship to God. Because they are signs, they also instruct. They not only presuppose faith, but by words and objects, they also nourish, strengthen, and express it. That is why they are called 'sacraments of faith'. They do, indeed, confer grace, but, in addition, the very act of celebrating them most effectively disposes the faithful to receive this grace to their profit, to worship God duly, and to practice charity" (SC 59).

1135-
1186

73. Who celebrates the liturgy?

While "in its full public worship is performed by the Mystical Body of Christ, that is, by the Head and his members" (SC 7), each individual member of the faithful has his own particular function. Through baptism, each Christian is rendered a part of the one royal priesthood of Jesus Christ. However, some are ordained by the sacrament of orders to represent Christ as Head of the Body.

1200-
1206

74. How should the liturgy be understood?

The "liturgy is made of unchangeable elements divinely instituted, and of elements subject to change. These latter not only may be changed but ought to be changed with the passage of time, if they have suffered from the intrusion of anything out of harmony with the inner nature of the liturgy or have become less suitable . . . both texts and rites should be drawn up so as to express more clearly the holy things they signify. The Christian people, as far as is possible, should be able to understand them with ease and take part in them fully, actively, and as a community" (SC 21).

Section II:

The Seven Sacraments of the Church

75. What is the sacrament of baptism?

1213-
1274

Baptism is the sacrament of spiritual rebirth. Through the symbolic action of washing with water and the use of the correct ritual formula ("I baptize you in the name of the Father, and of the Son, and of the Holy Spirit"), the baptized person is cleansed of all his sins and incorporated into Christ, becoming a member of the mystical Body and receiving all the graces of the supernatural life.

76. From where does the Church derive the sacrament of baptism?

The Church receives baptism from her Lord himself, who before ascending to his Father, entrusted this sacrament to his Church: "Full authority has been given to me both in heaven and on earth; go, therefore, and make disciples of all the nations. Baptize them in the name of the Father, and of the Son, and of the Holy Spirit" (Mt. 28:18-19).

77. Is baptism necessary for salvation?

Jesus Christ himself affirmed the necessity of baptism within the economy of salvation in his final instructions to his immediate disciples, which the early Church recalled in the Gospel of Mark: "Go into the whole world and proclaim the good news to all creation. The man who believes in it and accepts baptism will be saved;

the man who refuses to believe in it will be condemned" (Mk. 16:15-16). Thus, baptism is necessary for the salvation of those to whom the Gospel has been announced and who have the possibility of requesting this sacrament. The Church knows of no means other than baptism of assuring entrance into the eternal paradise. Nevertheless, it should be noted that while God has deigned to bind salvation with the sacrament of baptism, he is not himself bound to his sacraments. "For since Christ died for all, and since all men are in fact called to one and the same destiny, which is divine, we must hold that the Holy Spirit offers to all the possibility of being made partners, in a way known to God, in the paschal mystery" (GS 22). Therefore, the Church teaches that all men who, while ignorant of Christ and his Church, nevertheless seek truth and attempt to do the will of God according to their light, may be saved. It is supposed that such men of good will would have the explicit desire for baptism were they to be aware of its necessity.

1373-1381 78. What is the sacrament of confirmation?

Confirmation is the sacrament which perfects the graces of baptism through the seal of the Holy Spirit. "Incorporated into the Church by Baptism, the faithful are appointed by their baptismal character to Christian religious worship; reborn as sons of God, they must profess before men the faith they have received from God through the Church. By the sacrament of Confirmation they are more perfectly bound to the Church and are endowed with the special strength of the Holy Spirit. Hence they are, as true witnesses of Christ, more strictly obliged to spread the faith by word and deed" (LG 11).

79. Why is the sacrament of confirmation distinct from the sacrament of baptism?

As the very name "confirmation" implies, the sacrament of confirmation brings the sacrament of baptism to completion. The distinction between the two sacraments is found in the earliest of apostolic times: "When the apostles at Jerusalem heard that Samaria had accepted the word of God, they sent Peter and John to them. The two went down to these people and prayed that they might receive the Holy Spirit. It had not as yet come down upon any of them since they had been only baptized in the name of the Lord Jesus. The pair upon arriving imposed hands upon them and they received the Holy Spirit" (Acts 8:14-17).

80. What is the sacrament of the Eucharist?

1322-1372

The sacrament of the Eucharist is the heart and summit of the life of the Church in which Jesus Christ unites his Church to the one sacrifice offered to the Father on the altar of the Cross. In a manner of speaking, this sacrament is Jesus Christ himself since he offers himself, true God and true man, under the appearances of bread and wine. "By celebrating and also partaking in the Eucharist we unite ourselves with Christ on earth and in heaven who intercedes for us with the Father" (John Paul II, *Redemptor Hominis* 20).

81. When and why did Jesus Christ institute the sacrament of the Eucharist?

"At the Last Supper, on the night he was betrayed, our Savior instituted the eucharistic sacrifice of his Body and Blood. This he did in order to perpetuate the sacrifice of the Cross throughout the ages until he should come again, and so to entrust to his beloved Spouse, the Church, a memorial of his death and resurrection: a sacrament of love, a sign of unity, a bond of charity, a paschal banquet in which Christ is consumed, the mind is filled with grace, and a pledge of future glory is given to us" (SC 47).

1373-
1381
82. What does the Church believe about the presence of Jesus Christ in the sacrament of the eucharist?

The Church believes Jesus Christ is really and substantially present, in his Body and Blood, soul and divinity, when the bread and wine is changed by their consecration. The term for this real change is *transubstantiation*.

83. When does the transubstantiation of the bread and wine into the Body and Blood of Jesus Christ take place?

The transubstantiation of the bread and wine into the Body and Blood of Jesus Christ takes place during the Eucharist through the invocation of the Holy Spirit and the pronouncement of the words which the Lord himself spoke at the Last Supper: "This is my Body. . . . This is the cup of my Blood."

84. How long does Christ continue to be present in the sacrament of the Eucharist after the consecration?

Christ continues to be present under the species of bread and wine as long as the recognizable appearance of bread and wine remains.

1382-
1405
85. What are the conditions for receiving the sacrament of the Eucharist?

"Any baptized person who is not prohibited by law can and must be admitted to Holy Communion" (CIC, c. 912). All that is required is that "they have a sufficient knowledge and preparation so as to understand the mystery of Christ according to their capacity, and can receive the Body of the Lord with faith and devotion" (CIC, c. 913).

These canonical conditions for participation in the sacrament of the Eucharist can be understood in the light of St. Paul's emphasis on the need for a thorough examination of conscience, since "whoever eats the bread or drinks of the cup of the Lord unworthily sins against the body and blood of the Lord. A man should examine himself first; only then should he eat of the bread and drink of the cup" (1 Cor. 11:27-28). This means that those who are conscious of grave sin must first receive the sacrament of reconciliation before approaching to receive the sacrament of the Eucharist. Also, except the aged or infirm, anyone "who is to receive the Most Holy Eucharist is to abstain from food or drink, with the exception only of water or medicine, for at least the period of one hour before Holy Communion" (CIC, c. 919).

86. What is the sacrament of penance?

1422-1470

The sacrament of penance (also known as the sacrament of reconciliation) is the sacrament which accords pardon and forgiveness for those sins committed after baptism. "Those who approach the sacrament of penance obtain pardon from God's mercy for the offense committed against him, and are, at the same time, reconciled with the Church which they have wounded by their sins and which by charity, by example, and by prayer labors for their conversion" (LG 11).

87. From where does the Church receive its authority to forgive sins?

In sharing his power to forgive sins with his apostles, Jesus Christ also gave them the authority to reconcile sinners with the Church through forgiveness. This ecclesial dimension of reconciliation is especially highlighted in the solemn words of the Lord to Simon Peter: "I entrust to you the keys of the kingdom of heaven. Whatever you declare bound on earth shall be bound in heaven;

whatever you declare loosed on earth shall be loosed in heaven" (Mt. 16:19). "To the hands and the lips of the Apostles, his messengers, the Father mercifully entrusted a *ministry of reconciliation,* which they carry out in a singular way, by virtue of the power to act *in persona Christi* (John Paul II, *Reconciliatio et Paenitentia* 8).

88. What constitutes the sacrament of penance?

The sacrament of penance is constituted by the three acts of the penitent (repentance, the confession of sins to the priest, some form of manifestation of willingness to make reparation) and the sacramental absolution by the priest.

89. Why must sins be confessed to a priest?

The very act of confession of sins, even if viewed only from the human perspective, liberates the sinner and facilitates his reconciliation with others. Confession places the sinner face to face with his sins so that he can assume responsibility for them, and thus, he opens himself to the possibility of a new communion with God, the Church, and those around him.

90. Why is a penance imposed on the penitent?

The confessor imposes a penance on the penitent as a way towards repairing the damage caused by the sin as well as with a view towards the reestablishment of that conduct proper to a disciple of Christ.

91. What are the spiritual effects of the sacrament of penance?

The spiritual effects of the sacrament of penance are: reconciliation with God by which the penitent is restored to grace, reconciliation with the Church, the remission of the eternal punishment incurred by mortal sin, the remission (at least in part) of the temporal punishment of sins, peace and serenity of conscience, and an increase in the spiritual forces for Christian struggle.

92. What is an indulgence?

1471-1479

An indulgence is the "remission before God of the temporal punishment for sin, the guilt of which has already been forgiven, which a properly disposed member of the Christian faithful obtains under certain and definite conditions. It is granted by the Church which, as minister of redemption, authoritatively dispenses and applies the treasury of the merits of Christ and the saints" (Paul VI, *Indulgentiarum Doctrina*, 1-2).

93. What is the sacrament of anointing of the sick?

1499-1525

The sacrament of anointing of the sick confers a special grace for those who suffer from difficulties inherent to sickness or old age.

94. What are the effects of the sacrament of anointing of the sick?

The special grace of the sacrament of anointing of the sick has among its effects the union of the sick with the passion of Christ, the comforting and strengthening in faith of the sick, the forgiveness of sins in the case that the sick cannot receive the sacrament of penance, the restoration of health should this be for the sick's spiritual health, and the preparation for the journey into eternal life.

95. What is the sacrament of holy orders?

1536-1553

The sacrament of holy orders is the sacrament through which the mission entrusted by Christ to his apostles is continued in the Church until the end of time. "Christ, whom the Father hallowed and sent into the world, has, through his apostles, made their successors, the bishops, namely, sharers in his consecration and mission; and these, in their turn, duly entrusted in varying degrees various members of the Church with the office of their ministry. Thus the divinely instituted ecclesiastical ministry is exercised in different degrees by those who even from ancient times have been called bishops, priests, and deacons" (LG 28).

1554-
1561

96. What is a bishop?

A bishop receives the fullness of holy orders which makes him a member of the episcopal college and visible head of the particular church which is entrusted to him. Bishops, as successors of the apostles and members of the episcopal college, share in the apostolic responsibility for and mission of the entire Church under the authority of the Pope, successor of St. Peter.

1562-
1568

97. What is a priest?

A priest is one among those "prudent cooperators of the episcopal college and its support and mouthpiece, called to the service of the People of God, constitute, together with their bishop, a unique sacerdotal college (*presbyterium*) dedicated . . . to a variety of distinct duties" (LG 28). As priests, "on the level of their own ministry, sharing in the unique office of Christ, the mediator, they announce to all the word of God. However, it is in the eucharistic cult or in the eucharistic assembly of the people (*synaxis*) that they exercise in a supreme degree their sacred functions; there, acting in the person of Christ and proclaiming his mystery, they unite the votive offerings of the faithful to the sacrifice of Christ their head, and in the sacrifice of the Mass they make present again and apply, until the coming of the Lord, the unique sacrifice of the New Testament" (LG 28).

98. What is a deacon?

1569-
1571

A deacon is one of those who "receive the imposition of hands not unto the priesthood but unto the ministry. For, strengthened by sacramental grace they are dedicated to the People of God, in conjunction with the bishop and his body of priests, in the service of the liturgy, of the Gospel and of works of charity" (LG 29).

99. Who can receive the sacrament of holy orders?

1572-
1580

The clear teaching of the Church is that "only a baptized male validly receives sacred ordination" (CIC, c. 1024). The competent Church authority has the right and responsibility to call to holy orders those who show the proper aptitudes for the exercise of the ministry to which they aspire. In the Latin Church, the sacrament of priestly orders is generally only conferred on those candidates who freely and publicly embrace celibacy for the love of the kingdom of God and the service of men.

100. What are the effects of the sacrament of holy orders?

1581-
1589

"It is abundantly clear that by the imposition of hands and through the words of the consecration, the grace of the Holy Spirit is given, and a sacred character is impressed" (LG 21). Therefore, just as in the case of baptism and confirmation, the participation in the function of Christ is given once and for all time, likewise in the sacrament of holy orders, an *indelible spiritual character* is conferred which can neither be taken back nor conferred only temporarily.

101. What is the sacrament of matrimony?

1601-
1658

The sacrament of matrimony is the sacrament by which a man and a woman enter into an intimate life-long union by which "they signify and share the mystery of the unity and faithful love between Christ and the Church"

(LG 11). "The intimate partnership of life and the love which constitutes the married state has been established by the creator and endowed by him with its own proper laws: it is rooted in the contract of its partners, that is, in their irrevocable personal consent. It is an institution confirmed by the divine law and receiving its stability, even in the eyes of society, from the human act whereby the partners mutually surrender themselves to each other" (GS 48).

102. To what end is marriage ordained?

"For God himself is the author of marriage and has endowed it with various benefits and with various ends in view: all of these have a very important bearing on the continuation of the human race, on the personal development and destiny of every member of the family, and on the dignity, stability, peace, and prosperity of the family and of the whole human race. By its very nature, the institution of marriage and married love is ordered to procreation and education of the offspring and it is in them that it finds its crowning glory" (GS 48). Nevertheless, "marriage is not merely for the procreation of children: its nature as an indissoluble compact between two people and the good of the children demand that the mutual love of the partners be properly shown, that it should grow and mature. Even in cases where despite the intense desire of the spouses there are no children, marriage still retains its character of being a whole manner and communion of life and preserves its value and indissolubility" (GS 50).

1667-
1676   **103. What are sacramentals?**

Sacramentals are "sacred signs that bear a resemblance to the sacraments. They signify effects, particularly of a spiritual nature, which are obtained by the Church's intercession. By them men are disposed to receive the chief effect of the sacraments, and various occasions of life are rendered holy" (SC 60).

104. What is the purpose of a Christian funeral?

1680-
1690

A Christian funeral confers on the dead neither sacrament nor sacramental, since the dead have passed away from the sacramental economy of this life. Rather, the Christian funeral is a liturgical celebration which expresses the Church's communion with the dead at which the community assembles to both mourn him and to announce his passage to eternal life.

Part Three:
Life in Christ

Section I:

Man's Vocation: Life in the Spirit

105. What is the basis of the dignity of the human person?

"Christ the Lord, Christ the new Adam, in the very revelation of the mystery of the Father and of his love, reveals to man himself and brings to light his most high calling" (GS 22), that is, his creation, "in the image and likeness" (Gen. 1:27) of the Creator himself. Created with a spiritual and immortal soul, man is "the only creature on earth that God has wanted for its own sake" (GS 24) and is destined from conception for eternal happiness. Thus, the inherent dignity of the human person is based on man's place in the order of creation.

106. What are the beatitudes? 1716-1724

The beatitudes are at the heart of the message of Jesus Christ. Fulfilling the promises made by God since the covenant with Abraham and oriented towards the kingdom of heaven, they respond to the desire for blessedness which God has placed in each human heart. According to the Gospel of St. Matthew, the beatitudes are: "Blessed are the poor in spirit, for theirs is the kingdom of heaven. Blessed are those who mourn, for they shall be comforted. Blessed are the meek, for they shall inherit the earth. Blessed are those who hunger and thirst for righteousness, for they shall be satisfied. Blessed are the merciful, for they shall obtain mercy. Blessed are the pure of heart, for they shall see God. Blessed are the peacemakers, for they shall be called sons of God. Blessed are those who are persecuted for righteousness' sake, for theirs is the kingdom of heaven. Blessed are you when men revile you and persecute you and utter all kinds of evil against you falsely on my account. Rejoice and be glad, for your reward is great in heaven" (Mt. 5:3-12).

107. What is the purpose of human freedom?

"It is, however, only in freedom that man can turn himself toward what is good . . . that which is truly freedom is an exceptional sign of the image of God in man. For God willed that man 'be left in the hand of his own counsel' so that he might of his own accord seek his creator and freely attain his full and blessed perfection by cleaving to him. Man's dignity therefore requires him to act out of conscious and free choice, as moved and drawn in a personal way from within, and not by blind impulses in himself or by mere external constraint" (GS 17).

1749-
1756

108. What are the "sources" of the morality of human acts?

The "sources," or constitutive elements, of the morality of human acts are the object of the particular act, the intention of the act, and the circumstances of the act. The object of the act defines its morality according to reason which either judges it good or evil in itself. Evil acts cannot be justified by good intentions. Good acts, on the other hand, presuppose the goodness of the object, intention, and circumstances.

1762-
1770

109. What are the passions?

The passions are affections or sentiments, the principal among which include love and hate, desire and fear, joy, sadness, and anger. Being movements of the sensibilities, the passions are neither good nor bad in themselves. They can either be assumed into virtues or degenerate into vices.

110. What is the conscience?

The conscience is the judgment of reason whereby a human person recognizes the morality of a concrete act. "Deep within his conscience man discovers a law which he has not laid upon himself but which he must obey. Its voice, ever calling him to love and to do what is good and avoid evil, tells him inwardly at the right moment: do this, shun that. For man has in his heart a law inscribed by God. His dignity lies in observing this law, and by it he will be judged" (GS 16).

111. What is the role of the conscience in moral decisions?

Man must always obey the judgment of his conscience. This does not mean, however, that his conscience is always correct since it may be ignorant or erroneous in certain cases. This ignorance or error is not always free of fault. Rather, man has the obligation to correctly form his conscience according to the Word of God through faith, prayer, study, and practice.

112. What is a virtue?

1803-
1829

A virtue is the habitual and firm disposition to do what is good.

113. What are the human virtues?

The human virtues are the stable dispositions of the will and intellect which regulate human acts, order the passions, and guide conduct according to reason and faith. They can be summarized in the four cardinal virtues: prudence, justice, fortitude, and temperance.

114. What is the virtue of prudence?

The virtue of prudence disposes reason to the discernment of the true good and to the choice of the correct means to accomplish it.

115. What is the virtue of justice?

The virtue of justice consists in the constant resolution to give to God and to one's neighbor what is due to them.

116. What is the virtue of fortitude?

The virtue of fortitude assures, even in difficult circumstances, steadfastness and perseverance in the pursuit of the good.

117. What is the virtue of temperance?

The virtue of temperance moderates the attractions of sensible pleasures and facilitates a balance in the enjoyment of created things.

118. What are the theological virtues?

The theological virtues are those virtues which dispose a Christian to live in communion with the Holy Trinity. The theological virtues—faith, hope, and charity—have God for their origin, end, and object.

119. What is the virtue of faith?

The virtue of faith is that virtue whereby we believe in God and in all that the Church proposes to us for belief as coming from God.

120. What is the virtue of hope?

The virtue of hope disposes us to desire and await God with firm confidence in the eternal life.

121. What is the virtue of charity?

The virtue of charity leads us to love God above all else and to love our neighbor as ourselves for love of God.

It is the "bond of perfection" (Col. 3:14) between the other virtues.

122. What are the gifts of the Holy Spirit?

1830-1832

The gifts of the Holy Spirit are the permanent graces and dispositions which render man docile to following the impulses of the Spirit. Traditionally, they are seven in number: wisdom, understanding, counsel, fortitude, knowledge, piety, and fear of God.

123. What are the fruits of the Holy Spirit?

The fruits of the Holy Spirit are those perfections which are formed in man by the Spirit as a foretaste of eternal glory. The tradition of the Church numbers twelve of these fruits: "love, joy, peace, patience, kindness, goodness, mercy, gentleness, faithfulness, modesty, continence, and chastity" (Gal. 5:22-23, Vulgate).

124. What is a sin?

1846-1853

A sin is a word, act, or desire which is contrary to eternal law, and is, therefore, an offense against God. A sin, however, by its very nature is also against reason and, there, wounds both the sinner and his solidarity with his fellow men.

125. What is a mortal sin?

1854-1869

A mortal sin is to deliberately choose a grave matter which is contrary to the law of God or the true end of man. This choice destroys charity and renders eternal beatitude impossible. Unless a mortal sin is repented, it carries eternal death.

126. What is a venial sin?

A venial sin is a moral disorder which is nevertheless repairable by charity, which it leaves to subsist in man.

127. What are the "deadly sins"?

The "deadly sins" are those serious sins which tend to engender other sins and vices. Traditionally, the "deadly sins" are listed as seven in number: pride, greed, envy, anger, lust, gluttony, sloth.

128. What are the sins which "cry to heaven"?

In the Christian tradition, there are certain particularly grave sins which "cry to heaven" for justice (*peccata ad caelum clamantia*). These include homicide, oppression of the poor, sodomy, and resistance to grace.

1877-
1889
129. What is a society?

A society is a community of persons organically linked with each other by a principle of unity which is common to each of the members. Being both visible and spiritual, a society transcends barriers of time to embrace the past and the future. Human society is properly modelled on the divine society which is the Holy Trinity. "Insofar as man by his very nature stands completely in need of life in society, he is and he ought to be the beginning, the subject and the object of every social organization" (GS 25).

130. What is the principle of subsidiarity?

The principle of subsidiarity is a principle regarding social organization which has been embraced in the teachings of the recent Roman Pontiffs. Briefly stated, it holds that "a community of a higher order should not interfere in the interior life of a community of a lower order, depriving the latter of its functions, but rather should support it in case of need and help to coordinate its activity with the activities of the rest of society, always with a view to the common good" (John Paul II, *Centesimus Annus* 48).

131. What is the source of authority in society?

1897-1917

All human communities need an authority in order to maintain themselves and to develop properly. However, it must be noted that "there is no authority except from God, and all authority that exists is established by God" (Rom. 13:1). "It follows that political authority, either within the political community as such or through organizations representing the state, must be exercised within the limits of the moral order and directed towards the common good" (GS 74).

132. What is the "common good"?

The "common good" is defined as "the sum total of social conditions which allow people, either as groups or individuals, to reach their fulfillment more fully and more easily" (GS 26).

133. What is "social justice"?

1928-1942

The concept of "social justice" is intimately related to the common good and the exercise of authority. In a shortened definition, social justice can be understood as the concrete application of the common good by the competent authority.

134. What is a law?

1950-1953

A law is an "ordering of reason to the common good, promulgated by the one who has authority in the community" (St. Thomas Aquinas, *Summa Theologica* I-II, q. 90, art. 4).

135. What is natural law?

1954-1960

Natural law is that sum of norms regarding substantial values which is the necessary foundation for all other moral and civil norms. Since it is a participation in the wisdom and goodness of God by man who is formed in the image and likeness of his Creator, natural law is immutable through the course of history.

1961-
1964

136. What is the old law?

The old law is the first stage of revealed law, whose moral prescriptions are summarized in the Ten Commandments. This law, given to Moses on Mount Sinai, also contains many truths which are, in themselves, accessible to reason, but which God revealed directly since men failed to discern them in their hearts. The old law is also a preparation for the Gospel, which brings it to fulfillment.

1965-
1974

137. What is the new law?

The new law is the grace of the Holy Spirit, received through faith in Christ and operative through love. It is most clearly placed in relief in the Sermon on the Mount as well as in the seven sacraments of the Church. "This is because love, as the bond of perfection and fullness of the law, governs, gives meaning to, and perfects all the means of sanctification. Hence the true disciple of Christ is marked by love both of God and of his neighbor" (LG 42).

1987-
1995

138. What is justification?

Justification is the grace of the Holy Spirit which confers on us the justice of God. Uniting us by faith and baptism to the passion and resurrection of Jesus Christ, the Spirit brings us to a participation in the divine life. Justification, like conversion, presents two facets: through the action of grace, man freely turns towards God and away from sin, thereby receiving forgiveness and justification from above. Justification carries with it the remission of sins, the sanctification, and the interior renewal of the justified. We merit justification, which we receive in baptism, through the passion of Christ.

139. What is grace?

1996-2005

Grace is the assistance which God lends us in order that we may respond to our vocation to become his adopted children. It introduces us to intimacy with the trinitarian life. The divine initiative in the work of grace anticipates, prepares, and invites our free response.

140. What is merit?

2006-2011

The term "merit" is generally used to designate the retribution due to a community or society for the action of one of its members which is judged to be either good or bad and worthy of a recompense or sanction. However, as no man has merit before God, grace is a free gift of God.

141. What is the "call to holiness"?

2012-2016

The "call to holiness" means that "the followers of Christ, called by God not in virtue of their works but by his design and grace, and justified in the Lord Jesus, have been made sons of God in the baptism of faith and partakers of the divine nature, and so are truly sanctified. . . . It is therefore quite clear that all Christians in any state or walk of life are called to the fullness of Christian life and to the perfection of love, and by this holiness a more human manner of life is fostered also in earthly society" (LG 40).

142. What is the role of the Church in regard to the moral law?

2030-2046

The Church, having received the "solemn command of Christ from the apostles to announce the saving truth" (LG 17), has an important role in the guarding and transmission of the deposit of moral law and truth. "The Church has the right always and everywhere to proclaim moral principles, even in respect to the social order, and to make judgments about any human matter insofar as this is required by fundamental human rights or the salvation of souls" (CIC, c. 747). The Pope and bishops are "authentic teachers, that is, teachers endowed with the authority of Christ, to preach the faith to the people assigned to them, the faith which is destined to inform their thinking and direct their moral conduct" (LG 25). From the part of the members of the faithful, there is due a filial spirit towards this teaching office.

143. What are the Commandments of the Church?

The Commandments of the Church, traditionally six in number, are precepts which place the individual Christian's moral life in relief with the liturgical life of the Church, which in turn nourishes it. The six Commandments represent a sort of minimum indispensable level of rapport between the spirit of prayer and moral efforts. The six Commandments are: participation in the Eucharistic celebration on Sundays and Holy Days of Obligation, a minimum of an annual confession, the obligation to receive the Eucharist at least once a year during the Paschal season, the proper observation of feasts and holy days, the observation of days of fast and abstinence, and the obligation to assist with the material support of the Church and its works.

Section II:

The Ten Commandments

144. What moral good must we do in order to have eternal life? 2052-2074

In response to the young man who posed the same question, Jesus declared that it was necessary to recognize that "there is only One who is good," God himself. This said, the Lord affirmed that "if you wish to enter into life, keep the commandments" (Mt. 19:17).

145. What are the commandments?

The commandments of God, given to Israel through the teaching of Moses and summarized in the Decalogue (Ten Commandments), were brought to their perfection in the teaching of Jesus Christ, especially in the Sermon on the Mount. Since they express the fundamental obligations of man towards God and his neighbor, the Ten Commandments are binding for all times and places under grave obligation.

146. What is the basic moral message of the commandments?

Christ himself summarized the moral message of the commandments as: "'You shall love the Lord your God with your whole heart, with your whole soul, and with all your mind.' This is the greatest and first commandment. The second is like it: 'You shall love your neighbor as yourself.' On these two commandments the whole law is based, and the prophets as well" (Mt. 22:37-40). Traditionally, the first three commandments of the Decalogue have been associated with the first dominical command, love of God, while the other seven have been associated with the second dominical command, love of neighbor.

2084-
2132 ### 147. What is the First Commandment?

The First Commandment is: "I am the Lord your God, who brought you out of the land of Egypt, out of the house of bondage. You shall have no other gods before me. You shall not make for yourself a graven image, or any likeness of anything that is in heaven above, or that is in the earth beneath, or that is in the waters under the earth; you shall not bow down before them or serve them" (Ex. 20:2-5).

148. What are the moral teachings of the First Commandment?

The moral teaching of the First Commandment is that man should believe in God, hope in him, and love him above all else. Man has both a personal and social obligation to render to his Creator true worship and to fulfill any vows or promises made to him, whether in private or in public.

149. How does one sin against the First Commandment?

One sins against the First Commandment when one does not to pray to God or otherwise fails to give him the honor which is due to him. One also sins against this commandment by denying belief in God or by engaging in any sort of idolatry or superstition.

150. What is "atheism"?

The word "atheism" is used to signify several things which, although differing from each other considerably, share in somehow negating the true existence of God: "Some people expressly deny the existence of God. Others maintain that man cannot make any assertion whatsoever about him. Still others admit only such methods of investigation as would make it seem quite meaningless to ask questions about God . . . atheism, taken as a whole, is not present in the mind of man from the start. It springs from various causes, among which must be included a critical reaction against religions, and, in some places, against the Christian religion in particular" (GS 19).

151. What is the Church's attitude towards atheism?

While the Church cannot but absolutely reject atheism, she does not ignore some of its root causes for which "believers themselves often share responsibility" (GS 19). Thus, the Church recognizes that "atheism must be countered both by presenting true teaching in a fitting manner and by the full and complete life of the Church and of her members. For it is the function of the Church to render God the Father and his incarnate Son present and as it were visible, while ceaselessly renewing and purifying herself under the guidance of the Holy Spirit. This is brought about chiefly by the witness of a living and mature faith" (GS 21).

152. Does the cult of images in churches violate the First Commandment's ban on "graven images"?

The cult of images of our Lord and the saints in churches does not violate the First Commandment's ban on the worship of "graven images" since the Christian reverence of sacred images is a reverence towards the person they represent and not the image in itself. The reverent veneration given to images must be distinguished between the true worship (*latria*) which is due to God alone.

2142-
2159

153. What is the Second Commandment?

The Second Commandment is: "You shall not take the name of the Lord your God in vain" (Ex. 20:7).

154. What is the moral teaching of the Second Commandment?

The moral teaching of the Second Commandment prescribes respect for the name of the Lord, which is all-holy.

155. How does one sin against the Second Commandment?

One sins against the Second Commandment by misusing the name of God. Blasphemy, the light or facile use of the name of God, Jesus Christ, the Virgin Mary, or the saints, offends against the holiness of God. Perjury, the giving of false testimony under oath, offends against the faithfulness of God.

2168-
2189

156. What is the Third Commandment?

The Third Commandment is: "Remember the sabbath day, to keep it holy. Six days you shall labor, and do all your work; but the seventh day is the sabbath of the Lord your God; in it you shall not do any work" (Ex. 20:8-10).

157. What is the moral teaching of the Third Commandment?

The moral teaching of the Third Commandment is summarized in Church law: "Sunday, on which by apostolic tradition the paschal mystery is celebrated . . . and other holy days of obligation, the faithful are obliged to participate in the Mass. They are also to abstain from such work or business that would inhibit the worship to be given to God, the joy proper to the Lord's Day, or the due relaxation of mind and body" (CIC, cc. 1246-

1247). In addition to the religious reasons for this weekly observance of the sabbath, the Church is also mindful of the legitimate human reasons: "While devoting their time and energy to the performance of their work with a due sense of responsibility, workers should nevertheless be allowed sufficient rest and leisure to cultivate their family, cultural, social, and religious life. And they should be given the opportunity to develop those energies and talents, which perhaps are not catered for in their professional work" (GS 67).

158. How does one sin against the Third Commandment?

One sins against the Third Commandment by failing to participate at Mass on Sundays and holy days of obligation (or on their preceding evening vigils) or by engaging in needless work on such days.

159. What is the Fourth Commandment?

2197-
2246

The Fourth Commandment is: "Honor your father and your mother, that your days may be long in the land which the Lord your God gives you" (Ex. 20:12)

160. What is the moral teaching of the Fourth Commandment?

The moral teaching of the Fourth Commandment is that we should honor our parents as well as those who, for our own good, are in positions of authority over us.

161. What is the Christian family?

The human family was established by the Creator when he created man and woman. He endowed it with such a constitution that all of its members were to be persons equal in dignity although, for the common good, having different responsibilities. The Christian family in particular is "called to experience a new and original communion which confirms and perfects natural and human

communion. . . . The Christian family constitutes a specific revelation and realization of ecclesial communion,
and for this reason too it can and should be called the *domestic church*" (John Paul II, *FamiliarisConsortio* 21).

162. What are the duties of civil authorities?

The Fourth Commandment teaches us to honor those
who, for our own good, have received from God an
authority in society. It follows, therefore, that such
civil authorities must exercise their authority for the
benefit of the common good of those over whom they
have authority. This authority "must be exercised within
the limits of the moral order and directed towards the
common good (understood in the dynamic sense of the
term) according to the juridical order legitimately established" (GS 74).

163. What are the duties of a Christian in public society?

In public society, the Christian insofar as he is a citizen
is obliged in conscience to observe the legitimate regu-
lations of civil authorities so long as these are not contrary to the norms of the moral order since "it is better
for us to obey God than men" (Acts 5:29). This principle being understood, "Citizens should cultivate a
generous and loyal spirit of patriotism, but without
narrow-mindedness. . . . Christians must be conscious
of their specific and proper role in the political community: they should be a shining example by their sense
of responsibility and their dedication to the common
good; they should show in practice how authority can
be reconciled with freedom, personal initiative and with
the solidarity and the needs of the whole social frame-
work" (GS 75).

2258-
2317
164. What is the Fifth Commandment?

The Fifth Commandment is: "You shall not kill" (Ex.
20:13).

165. What is the moral teaching of the Fifth Commandment?

The moral teaching of the Fifth Commandment is that all human life, from the moment of conception to the moment of death, is sacred because the human person is of value in and of himself as a being created in the image and likeness of the living and holy God. Therefore, any form of murder or unjust taking of human life is an offense against the dignity of humanity and the holiness of the Creator.

166. How does one sin against the Fifth Commandment?

One sins against the Fifth Commandment by murder, suicide, abortion, and any other violence against human life, as well as by scandal.

167. What is murder?

Murder is the willful and unjust taking of a human life.

168. How does the murder apply to abortion?

From its conception, a child has the same right to life as any other human person. Direct abortion is an "abominable crime" (GS 51) which is gravely against moral law and is punished by the Church with the sanction of excommunication.

169. What is euthanasia?

Euthanasia is an act or an omission which is intended to bring about the death of an aged or infirm person. Notwithstanding any possible good intentions, euthanasia is an act of murder, which offends both against the human person and against God the Creator of life.

170. Why is voluntary suicide wrong?

Voluntary suicide is wrong because it is a sin against life which offends against justice, hope, and charity.

171. What is scandal?

Scandal is when one, either through deliberate action or omission, causes another to sin. It is a sin against the Fifth Commandment since it offends against the sanctity of life. "Scandals may inevitably arise, but woe to him through whom they come. He would be better off thrown into the sea with a millstone around his neck than giving scandal to one of these little ones" (Lk. 17:1-2).

172. Does the Fifth Commandment forbid war?

As the Fifth Commandment forbids the voluntary taking of human life, individuals and governments are obliged to avoid war insofar as possible. Nevertheless, "as long as the danger of war persists and there is no international authority with the necessary competence and power, governments cannot be denied the right of lawful self-defense, once all peace efforts have failed" (GS 79).

2331-
2391
173. What is the Sixth Commandment?

The Sixth Commandment is: "You shall not commit adultery" (Ex. 20:14).

174. What is the moral teaching of the Sixth Commandment?

The moral teaching of the Sixth Commandment is based on the truth that "God created man in his image; in the divine image he created him; male and female he created them" (Gen. 1:27). Furthermore, "God is love and in Himself He lives a mystery of personal loving communion. Creating the human race in his own image and continually keeping it in being, God inscribed in the humanity of man and woman the vocation, and thus the capacity and responsibility, of love and communion" (John Paul II, *Familiaris Consortio* 11). Therefore, each man and woman is called to recognize and to accept his or her sexual identity as a gift from God which should be well-ordered towards the end for which it was created, that is, authentic love and communion.

175. How does one sin against the Sixth Commandment?

One sins against the Sixth Commandment through acts which are contrary to authentic love and the true end of the gift of human sexuality. These acts include adultery, sensuality, masturbation, fornication, pornography, prostitution, rape, and homosexual acts. Also, thoughts of sexual impurity are also sinful against the Sixth Commandment.

176. Why are thoughts of sexual impurity sinful against the Sixth Commandment?

Thoughts of sexual impurity are sinful against the Sixth Commandment because the human person is a unity which cannot be divided. Mental purity cannot be artificially separated from physical purity. Jesus himself taught a rigorous interpretation of the Sixth Commandment: "You have heard the commandment, 'You shall not commit adultery.' What I say to you is: anyone who looks lustfully at a woman has already committed adultery with her in his thoughts" (Mt. 5:27-28).

177. What is chastity?

Chastity is the successful integration of sexuality within the context of the human person through the interior unity achieved between his corporal and spiritual being. Through chastity, sexuality, which belongs to the corporal and biological dimension of man, is personalized and rendered truly human in a person-to-person relation. Thus chastity implies both the integrity of the gift of the sexuality and the integrity of the human person.

178. What is the Church's attitude towards homosexual activity?

The term "homosexuality" refers to sexual attraction and relations between men or women with persons of the same sex. Supported by Sacred Scripture, the Tradition of the Church has always held that "homosexual acts are intrinsically disordered" (Congregation for the Doctrine of the Faith, *Persona humana* 8) and against the natural law since these sexual acts are closed to the gift of life and do not proceed from an true affective and sexual complementarity. Homosexual persons are called to live a life of chastity and can achieve sanctification through the union of their difficulties with the sacrifice of the Cross.

179. What are the ends of marriage?

The ends of marriage are the good of the two spouses themselves and the transmission of life. This "teaching, often set forth by the Magisterium, is founded upon the inseparable connection, willed by God and unable to be broken by man on his own initiative, between the two meanings of the conjugal act: the unitive meaning and the procreative meaning" (Paul VI, *Humanae Vitae* 12). One cannot separate these two meanings of the values of marriage without inflicting damage to the spiritual life of the couple and compromising the goods of the marriage and family.

180. Why is divorce contrary to the sense of the Sixth Commandment?

Divorce is contrary to the sense of the Sixth Commandment because it attempts to break a freely entered contract which the two partners made with each other for life. It offends against the covenant of salvation which sacramental marriage is a preeminent sign.

181. What is the Seventh Commandment?

2401-2449

The Seventh Commandment is: "You shall not steal" (Ex. 20:15).

182. What is the moral teaching of the Seventh Commandment?

The moral teaching of the Seventh Commandment prescribes the practice of justice and charity in the use of the goods of the earth and the fruits of human labor. The goods of creation being destined for the whole human race, the right to private property cannot be absolutized to the detriment of the common good. "God destined the earth and all it contains for all men and all peoples so that all created things would be shared fairly by all mankind under the guidance of justice tempered by charity. No matter what the structures of property are in different peoples, according to various and changing circumstances and adapted to their lawful institutions, we must never lose sight of this universal destination of earthly goods. Therefore every man has the right to possess a sufficient amount of the earth's goods for himself and his family" (GS 69).

183. How does one sin against the Seventh Commandment?

One sins against the Seventh Commandment when one steals or otherwise usurps the goods or property of another contrary to the reasonable will of the owner. Any unjust use of the goods of another is a sin against the Seventh Commandment and the injustice requires reparation.

184. How does the "universal destination of earthly goods" apply to the environment?

The Seventh Commandment, in general, and the principle of the "universal destination of earthly goods," in particular, oblige us to respect the integrity of creation. Animals, plants, and inanimate elements, are destined for the common good of humanity past, present, and future. Their use, therefore, must nor be detached from this moral exigency.

185. What is the role of the Church in regard to social doctrine?

The Church receives from the Gospel the full revelation of the truth of man. Therefore, "Christian revelation . . . promotes deeper understanding of the laws of social living with which the Creator has endowed man's spiritual and moral nature" (GS 23). While the Church does not exclusively embrace any one system of social or economic organization, it reserves the right to pass judgment on all of them "whenever the fundamental rights of man or the salvation of souls requires it" (GS 76).

186. What is the teaching of the Church in regard to contemporary systems of social and economic organization?

In regard to contemporary systems of social and economic organization, the Church rejects totalitarian schemes and the atheism which is usually associated with them, especially in their "communist" and "socialist" manifestations. On the other hand, the Church refrains from embracing the type of "capitalism" which is characterized by individualism and the supremacy of the law of the market vis-à-vis human work. The regulation of the economy according to centralized planning perverts basic social bonds, while the regulation by the so-called "law of the market" often leads to a lack of social justice. Therefore, the social doctrine of the Church has tended to favor a reasonable market economy with freedom for economic initiative, but tempered by a hierarchy of values with the common good in mind.

187. What is the role of the state in social and economic organization?

The Church recognizes that the state has an important role to play in social and economic organization: "Economic activity, especially the activity of a market economy, cannot be conducted in an institutional, juridical or political vacuum. On the contrary, it presupposes sure guarantees of individual freedom and private property, as well as a stable currency and efficient public services. Hence the principal task of the State is to guarantee this security, so that those who work and produce can enjoy the fruits of their labors and thus feel encouraged to work efficiently and honestly. . . . Another task of the State is that of overseeing and directing the exercise of human rights in the economic sector. However, primary responsibility in this area belongs not to the State but to individuals and to the various groups which make up society" (John Paul II, *Centesimus Annus* 48).

188. What is the Eighth Commandment?

2464-
2503

The Eighth Commandment is: "You shall not bear false witness against your neighbor" (Ex. 20:16).

189. What is the moral teaching of the Eighth Commandment?

The moral teaching of the Eighth Commandment is founded on the truthfulness God "whose fidelity endures from age to age" (Ps. 119:90). Thus the faithful are called to "put on the new man created in God's image, whose justice and holiness are born of truth" (Eph. 4:24). Thus the moral teaching of the Eighth

Commandment calls all men to live according to the truth, that virtue which consists of truthfulness in all words and actions and which guards against all duplicity, simulation, and hypocrisy.

190. How does one sin against the Eighth Commandment?

One sins against the Eighth Commandment by lies, calumny, detraction, and other forms of deceit.

191. What is the relationship between truth and beauty?

Truth is beautiful in itself, for it "is an aura of the might of God and a pure effusion of the glory of the Almighty" (Wis. 7:25). Furthermore, God reveals himself through the beauty—that is, the order and harmony—of the universe since "from the greatness and the beauty of created things their original author is, by analogy, seen" (Wis. 13:5). "Created in the image of God" (Gen. 1:26), man likewise expresses truth through the beauty of his artistic works. The arts, therefore, are a particular human expression which serve to manifest the interior riches of man. The sacred arts are true and beautiful when they are faithful to their vocation, which is that "of their nature the arts are directed toward expressing in some way the infinite beauty of God in works made by human hands. Their dedication to the increase of God's praise and of his glory is more complete, the more exclusively they are devoted to turning men's minds devoutly toward God" (SC 122).

2514-
2527

192. What is the Ninth Commandment?

The Ninth Commandment is: "You shall not covet your neighbor's house; you shall not covet your neighbor's wife, or his manservant, or his maidservant, or his ox, or anything that is your neighbor's" (Ex. 20:17).

193. What is the moral teaching of the Ninth Commandment?

The moral teaching of the Ninth Commandment is to place us on guard against jealousy and every sort of material covetousness. The struggle against the vice of jealousy is accomplished through purification of the heart and the cultivation of the virtue of temperance.

194. How do we purify our hearts?

We can purify our hearts through constant prayer, the regular practice of chastity and modesty, and by careful guard of our intentions. However, in the end, "no man can master himself unless God grant it" (Wis. 8:21, Vulgate).

195. What is the Tenth Commandment?

2534-2550

The Tenth Commandment is: "You shall not covet . . . anything that is your neighbor's" (Ex. 20:17) and "neither shall you covet your neighbor's wife; and you shall not desire your neighbor's house, his field, or his manservant, or his maidservant, his ox, or his ass, or anything that is your neighbor's" (Dt. 5:21).

196. What is the moral teaching of the Tenth Commandment?

The moral teaching of the Tenth Commandment repeats and complements that of the Ninth Commandment, which emphasized the carnal aspects of concupiscence. It censures that jealousy of the goods of another, which is at the root of all crime and fraud, which are forbidden by the Seventh Commandment. It bans the "coveting with the eyes" which so often leads to the violence and injustice forbidden by the Fifth Commandment. It likewise bans lustfulness, which leads to the sins censured by the Sixth Commandment, as well as cupidity, censured by the first three precepts of the

Decalogue. Thus in a sense, the moral teaching of the Ninth and Tenth Commandments summarize the precepts of the entire law.

Part Four:
Prayer in Christian Life

Section I:

Prayer in
Christian Life

197. What is prayer?
2558-
2565

Prayer is the "lifting up of the heart to God or the seeking from God of reasonable goods" (St. John Damascene, *De fide orthodoxa* 3:24). Prayer is a gift from God since, by ourselves, "in our weakness we do not know how to pray as we ought" (Rom. 8:26).

198. What is the place of prayer in the Old Testament?
2568-
2589

Although scripture scholars point out that the Old Testament does not have a generalized concept of prayer *per se*, the entirety of the Old Testament is nevertheless replete with examples of prayer as the bond between God and the unfolding events of human history. The prayer of Abraham and Jacob is presented as a struggle of faith characterized both by a confidence in the fidelity of God and a certainty of the victory promised to perseverance. The prayer of Moses responds to the initiative of the living God for the salvation of his people and prefigures the later prayer of intercession of the sole mediator, Jesus Christ. The prayer of the entire people of God developed in the context of his presence in the ark of the covenant and the temple. The prayer of the prophets sought the conversion of the people and yearned to see the face of God. Finally, the psalms are the most evident prayer in the Old Testament, uniting as they do both individual and community prayer. Prayed by Christ himself, the psalms are today an essential element of the prayer of the Church, adapted to the needs of men of all times and conditions.

2598- **199. What does Jesus Christ teach about prayer in the New**
2616   **Testament?**

Jesus Christ is himself the perfect model of prayer in the New Testament. Retreating often into solitude in order to commune with his heavenly Father, Jesus enjoyed in his prayer a loving union with the will of the Father, a union which continued onto the Cross itself. It was because of this very example that his disciples asked for his teaching on prayer: "One day he was praying in a certain place. When he had finished, one of his disciples asked him: 'Lord, teach us to pray. . . . '" (Lk. 11:1). In his teaching, Jesus taught his disciples to pray with a pure heart, a living and persistent faith, and a filial daring. He called on them to keep vigilant with their prayer and to present their needs to God in his name.

2617- **200. What is the role of the prayer of Virgin Mary in the**
2619   **New Testament?**

The prayer of the Virgin Mary reveals the dawn of the fullness of time. Before the Incarnation, her prayerful union with God carried to fulfillment the designs of the Father. Before the outpouring of the Spirit on Pentecost, her prayer assisted in preparing for the formation of the Church. Her simple reply of faith to the angel Gabriel—"I am the servant of the Lord. Let it be done to me as you say" (Lk. 1:38)—is the synthesis of the content of Christian prayer. Thus, "the Virgin Mother is constantly present on this journey of faith of the People of God toward the light. This is shown in a special way by the canticle of the *Magnificat*, which having welled up from the depths of Mary's faith at the Visitation, ceaselessly re-echoes in the heart of the Church down the centuries" (John Paul II, *Redemptoris Mater* 35).

2623- **201. From where does the Church derive her life of prayer?**
2643

On Pentecost, the Holy Spirit was poured forth on the nascent Church to instruct her and to recall to her all that her Lord had taught. This same Spirit also guided her in her development of the general forms of prayer.

202. What are the general forms of prayer in the life of the Church?

The general forms of prayer in the life of the Church are the prayers of blessing and adoration, petition, intercession, thanksgiving, and praise.

203. What is the prayer of blessing and adoration?

The prayer of blessing and adoration is at the heart of the meeting of God and man which is prayer itself. The prayer of blessing and adoration is the result of the recognition of God by man in this encounter and is the response of man to the free gift of God: "Come, let us sing joyfully to the Lord . . . let us greet him with thanksgiving" (Ps. 95:1-2).

204. What is the prayer of petition?

The prayer of petition is the form of prayer which has for its objects the forgiveness of our sins, the desire for the kingdom of God, and the request for our legitimate needs since "we will receive at his hands whatever we ask" (1 Jn. 3:22).

205. What is the prayer of intercession?

The prayer of intercession, as different from the prayer of petition, seeks after the good of others without distinction since Christian love impels us to each "look after the interests of others rather than his own" (Phil. 2:4).

206. What is the prayer of thanksgiving?

The prayer of thanksgiving gives thanks to God for all the events of our lives, whether they be joys or sorrows, since we are called to "rejoice always, never cease praying, render constant thanks; such is God's will for you in Christ Jesus" (1 Th. 5:16-18).

207. What is the prayer of praise?

The prayer of praise is the form of prayer which most directly recognizes God as God. It sings his praise for himself, it glorifies him not so much because of what he has done, but because of who he is. The prayer of praise participates in the beatitude of those hearts who loved God in faith even before they saw him in his glory. The prayer of praise unites the other forms of prayer and brings them, in the Spirit, to him who is the source and end of all of them: the "one God, the Father, from whom all things come and for whom we live; and one Lord Jesus Christ, through whom everything was made and through whom we live" (1 Cor. 8:6).

2652- 208. What are the sources of the Church's prayer?
2660

The Spirit teaches the Church her prayer through the transmission of Tradition. This tradition has handed down to the Church as sources of prayer: the Word of God, the liturgy of the Church, and the virtues of faith, hope, and charity.

2663- 209. What is the place of the Trinity in Christian prayer?
2679

Christian prayer is above all a Trinitarian prayer. It is primarily addressed to the Father through the mediation of the Son. However, as "no one can say 'Jesus is Lord' except in the Holy Spirit" (1 Cor. 12:3), Christian prayer also invokes the Spirit as the true master of prayer.

2683- 210. What are the guides for the prayer of the Church?
2691

In her prayer, the pilgrim Church communes with, seeks intercession from, and takes her example from the saints, among whom the Mother of God is most prominent. The different schools of spirituality in the Christian tradition also serve as precious guides for the life of prayer. The ordained ministers of the Church as well as those with other public functions in the Church also aid her members in the development of their lives of prayer. However, before any of these, it is the family which is the first guide to any individual Christian's prayer. "In what might be regarded as the domestic Church, the parents, by word and example, are the first heralds of the faith with regard to their children" (LG 11).

211. What is the role of prayer in the life of the the individual Christian?   2697-2719

The Church invites the individual Christian to make prayer a regular part of every aspect of his life rhythm through daily prayer, the Liturgy of the Hours, the Sunday Eucharist, and the feasts throughout the liturgical year.

212. What are the principal expressions of the life of prayer?

In the Christian tradition, there are three principal expressions of the life of prayer: vocal prayer, meditation, and contemplation.

213. What is vocal prayer?

Vocal prayer, which is founded upon the union of body and spirit in the human nature, associates the body with the interior prayer of the soul through the use of words and other expressions.

214. What is meditation?

Meditation is, above all, a prayerful search which opens the heart, imagination, emotions, and desire to the message of God contained in the mysteries of Christ, as is preeminently accessible to those who use the *lectio divina* or the rosary.

215. What is contemplation?

Contemplation, or mental prayer, is the simplest expression of prayer. It is the type of prayer which searches for "he whom my heart loves" (S. of S. 1:7), that is, Jesus and, in him, the Father. Contemplation has its view fixed upon Jesus, and him as the Word of God, in silent love and seeks to make us a participant in his very mystery.

2725-2752

216. What is meant by the term "struggle in prayer"?

The term "struggle in prayer" refers to the fact that prayer necessarily supposes a struggle against ourselves and against the devices of the enemy. This struggle is inseparable from the daily struggle of the spiritual life in general since one prays as one lives and one lives as one prays.

217. What are the common difficulties in prayer life?

The two most common difficulties in a life of prayer are distraction and "spiritual dryness," that is, periods when prayer seemingly does not carry with it a sense of "well-being" or satisfaction.

218. What are the remedies for difficulties in prayer?

Difficulties in prayer can be greatly remedied by perseverance, faith, conversion, and vigilance.

219. What is the "Prayer of the Hour of Jesus"?

The "Prayer of the Hour of Jesus" is the prayer which the Lord addressed to his heavenly Father before his passion. Found in the Seventeenth chapter of the Gospel of St. John, where it is also known as the "Sacerdotal Prayer," this prayer of Jesus Christ summarizes the entire economy of creation and salvation. It is in this prayer that the Lord fully reveals himself to us and, in so doing, reveals the Father: "Just Father, the world has not known you, but I have known you; and these men have known that you sent me. To them I have revealed your name, and I will continue to reveal it so that your love for me may live in them and I may live in them" (Jn. 17:25-26).

Section II:

The Lord's Prayer: "Our Father"

220. What is the "Lord's Prayer"?   2759-
                                                          2772
In response to the request of his disciples that he should
teach them to pray "as John taught his disciples" (Lk.
11:1), Jesus taught them the prayer which has come to
be known as the "Lord's Prayer." In the tradition of the
liturgy of the Church, the fuller text is found in the
Gospel of St. Matthew: "Our Father who art in heaven,
hallowed be thy name. Thy kingdom come. Thy will
be done, on earth as it is in heaven. Give us this day our
daily bread; and forgive us our debts, as we also have
forgiven our debtors; and lead us not into temptation,
but deliver us from evil" (Mt. 6:9-13).

221. Why is this prayer called the "Lord's Prayer"?

This prayer has been traditionally called the "Lord's
Prayer" because it has been given to us by the Lord
Jesus himself and is unique in that regard among all
other prayers. Furthermore, this prayer summarizes
the teachings on prayer of Jesus Christ, who is himself
the model *par excellence* for our prayer life.

222. What is the doxology of the Lord's Prayer?

The doxology of the Lord's prayer consists of the words
of praise which the liturgy adds to the end of the Lord's
Prayer. Already in the Church's first century, the *Didache* added the phrase "for thine is the power and the
glory forever" (*Didache* 8:2). The *Apostolic Constitutions*

added "the kingdom" to this doxology, rendering it into the form by which it is known today. Although the doxology is not properly a part of the Lord's prayer, it does enjoy a certain status due to its long tradition of use in the Church's liturgy and in ecumenical prayer.

223. What is the importance of the Lord's Prayer?

The importance of the Lord Prayer derives from the fact that "if we pray rightly and fittingly, we can say nothing else but what is contained in this prayer" (St. Augustine, *Epistulae (ad Probam)* 133:12). If all of Scripture—the Law, the prophets, and the psalms—are fulfilled in Christ, then it follows that his prayer is the culmination of all prayer. "The Lord's prayer is most perfect . . . in the Lord's Prayer not only do we ask for all that we may rightly desire, but also in order wherein we ought to desire them, so that this prayer not only teaches us to ask, but also directs our affections" (St. Thomas Aquinas, *Summa Theologica* II-II, q. 83, art. 9).

224. How is the Lord's Prayer the prayer of the Church?

The Lord's Prayer is truly *the* prayer of the Church. It forms an integral part of the major hours of the Divine Office as well as of the sacraments of Christian initiation: baptism, confirmation, and the Eucharist. Within the context of the Eucharistic celebration, the Lord's Prayer takes on an eschatological dimension as its petitions are made in the hope of the Lord "until he comes" (1 Cor. 11:26).

2777- ### 225. To whom is the Lord's Prayer addressed?
2785
The Lord's Prayer is addressed to God as "Father."

226. Why does the Lord's Prayer address God "Father"?

We "dare," as the liturgy reminds us, to address God as "Father" because that is how he revealed himself to us through his Son who became man and through his Spirit who helps us to recognize him: "The Spirit himself gives witness with us that we are children of God" (Rom. 8:16).

227. What do we mean when we invoke God as "Our Father"? 2786-2793

In invoking God as "Our Father," we evoke the New Covenant in Jesus Christ, the communion with the Holy Trinity, and the divine love—all of which the Church mediates to the world.

228. What does the expression "who art in heaven" mean? 2794-2796

The expression "who art in heaven" does not refer to a place but to the very majesty of God and his presence in the souls of the just. "Heaven" also refers to the dwelling place of the Father to where, as members of the People of God, "we have already been given a place" (Eph. 2:6) even if we still "groan while we are here, even as we yearn to have our heavenly habitation envelop us" (2 Cor. 5:2).

229. What are the "seven petitions" of the Lord's Prayer? 2803-2806

Traditionally, after the initial address to the Father, the Lord's prayer has been divided into "seven petitions," three of which "will be perfectly fulfilled in the life to come, the other four . . . belong to the needs of the present" (St. Thomas Aquinas, *Summa Theologica* II-II, q. 83, art. 9). The first three petitions—the sanctification of the name, the coming of the kingdom, and the fulfillment of the divine will—have for the object the glory of the Father. In contrast, the other four petitions—our daily sustenance, the forgiveness of our sins, the avoidance of temptation, and the deliverance from evil—present our most basic needs to the Father.

2807- **230. What is the meaning of the first petition of the Lord's
2815   Prayer, "hallowed be thy name"?**

The first petition of the Lord's Prayer, "hallowed by thy name," is not meant in a causal sense since God alone is holy and, thus, he alone has the power to sanctify. The holiness of God is the inaccessible dwelling of his own eternal mystery. Nevertheless, in his condescending mercy, God "has given us the wisdom to understand fully the mystery" (Eph. 1:9) and thus we are called to be "holy and blameless in his sight" (Eph. 1:4). Thus, by the invocation "hallowed be thy name," we enter into an active participation of with the divine plan of revelation and sanctification.

231. What is the name of God?

In the Old Testament, the name of God was revealed to Moses and preserved in the ineffable tetragrammaton YHWH. In the fullness of time, however, God manifested himself and his name in a most intimate way in his incarnate Son who revealed God as Father.

2816- **232. What is the meaning of the second petition of the Lord's
2821   Prayer, "thy kingdom come"?**

The second petition of the Lord's Prayer, "thy kingdom come," prays above all for the definitive coming of the kingdom of God through the coming of Jesus Christ in glory.

233. How does the eager anticipation of the coming kingdom of God effect the Church's view towards the present world?

While the Church looks forward with eager anticipation to the eschatological fulfillment of the kingdom of God, this does not mean that it is unconcerned with the present world. The Christian's vocation to eternal life, rather than distracting, actually reinforces his responsibilities in the present life. "We know neither the moment of the consummation of the earth and of man nor the way the universe will be transformed. The form of this world, distorted by sin, is passing away and we are taught that God is preparing a new dwelling and a new earth in which righteousness dwells. . . . Far from diminishing our concern to develop this earth, the expectancy of a new earth should spur us on, for it is here that the body of a new human family grows, foreshadowing in some way the age which is to come. . . . When we have spread on the earth the fruits of our nature and our enterprise—human dignity, fraternal communion, and freedom—according to the command of the Lord and in his Spirit, we will find them once again, cleansed this time from the stain of sin, illuminated and transfigured" (GS 39).

234. What is the meaning of the third petition of the Lord's Prayer, "Thy will be done, on earth as it is in heaven"? 2822-2827

The third petition of the Lords's Prayer prays that our will might be united to that of the Father in order that his salvific plan might be advanced among men.

235. What is the will of the Father?

The will of the Father is that "all men might be saved and come to know the truth" (1 Tm. 2:4). It is for this reason that "God has given us the wisdom to understand fully the mystery, the plan he was pleased to decree in Christ, to be carried out in the fullness of time: namely, to bring all things in the heavens and on the earth into one under Christ's headship. In him we were chosen, for in the decree of God, who administers everything according to his will" (Eph. 1:9-11).

236. How is the will of God "done"?

The will of God was "done" perfectly once and for all time by Jesus Christ, through his human will. Upon entering this world, the Son declared: "Behold, I come to do your will" (Heb. 10:7). Throughout his life, Jesus has as his constant principle: "I do nothing on my own authority" (Jn. 8:28). Finally, in the prayer of his agony, he entrusted himself entirely to the will of the Father: "Yet not my will, but yours" (Lk. 22:42). Thus, it is truly "by this 'will' we have been sanctified through the offering of the body of Jesus Christ once for all" (Heb. 10:10).

237. How do we fulfill the will of the Father?

By ourselves, we are wholly incapable of doing the will of the Father. However, united with Jesus Christ in the power of the Holy Spirit, we can entrust to him our own wills and choose what the Son always chose: to do the what is pleasing to the Father. Through prayer, we can "discern what is the will of God" (Rom. 12:2) and obtain the "patience to do God's will" (Heb. 10:36). In this regard, we share in the confidence that while "God does not hear sinners, if someone is devout and obeys his will, he listens to him" (Jn. 9:31).

2828- 238. What is the meaning of the fourth petition of the Lord's
2837   Prayer, "Give us this day our daily bread"?

In the fourth petition of the Lord's prayer, we express, in communion with all our brothers and sisters, our filial confidence ("Give us") that our heavenly Father will provide us with not only the nourishment necessary for our earthly life ("our daily bread") but also that nourishment for our eternal life which is the Word of God and the Body of Christ.

239. **What is the meaning of the fifth petition of the Lord's** 2838-
Prayer, "And forgive us our debts, as we have also 2845
forgiven our debtors"?

The fifth petition of the Lord's Prayer asks God's forgiveness for our sins. However, his forgiveness cannot penetrate into our hearts if we do not ourselves forgive those who have sinned against us according to example and with the help of Christ.

240. **What is the relationship between Christian love and forgiveness?**

Christ taught that "I give you a new commandment: Love one another. Such as my love has been for you, so must your love be for each other. This is how all will know you for my disciples: your love for one another" (Jn. 13:34-35). It is impossible to observe this commandment apart from the divine model and in active communion with him. When mankind was steeped in sin, God, "the Father of mercies, through death and resurrection of his Son reconciled the world to himself and sent the Holy Spirit among us for the forgiveness of sins" (Ritual of Penance, Formula of Absolution). Thus, as children who have been reconciled to the Father through this great love, we must "forgive one another as God in Christ forgave us" (Eph. 4:32). Otherwise, we risk that our "heavenly Father will treat you in exactly the same way unless each of you forgives his brother with his heart" (Mt. 18:35).

241. **What is the meaning of the sixth petition of the Lord's** 2846-
Prayer, "lead us not into temptation"? 2849

The sixth petition of the Lord's Prayer asks God not to permit us to fall into the path which leads to sin and prays for the Spirit of discernment and fortitude. This petition also asks for the grace of vigilance and final perseverance.

242. Does God test us with temptation?

"No one who is tempted is free to say, 'I am being tempted by God.' Surely God, who is beyond the grasp of evil tempts no one. Rather the tug and lure of his own passion tempt every man. Once passion has conceived, it gives birth to sin, and when sin reaches maturity it begets death" (Jas. 1:13-15). God, on the contrary, seeks to free us from sin and gives us his gift of discernment if we ask for it in faith.

2850- 243. What is the meaning of the seventh petition of the
2854   Lord's Prayer, "but deliver us from evil"?

In the seventh and final petition of the Lord's Prayer, "but deliver us from evil," we unite with the Church to implore God to manifest his victory—the victory already won by Jesus Christ—over the "prince of this world" (Jn. 14:30), Satan, the fallen angel who personally opposes God and his divine plan of salvation.

244. When was this the victory over "the prince of this world" won?

The the victory over "the prince of this world" was won when Jesus freely handed himself over to death in order to give us his life. It was of this moment that Scripture records that "now has judgment come upon this world, now will this world's prince be driven out, and I—once I am lifted up from the earth—will draw all men to myself" (Jn. 12:31-32).

245. What other meaning does the petition "but deliver us from evil" have?

The seventh petition of the Lord's Prayer also asks God for deliverance from all the evils—past, present, and future—which are indirectly caused by the evil one. It is with a view towards the eschatological coming of Christ when the present woes will finally be ended that the Church implores the Father at every Eucharistic celebration: "Deliver us, Lord, from every evil, and grant us peace in our day. In your mercy keep us free from sin and protect us from all anxiety as we wait in joyful hope for the coming of our Savior, Jesus Christ" (Roman Missal, Embolism).

246. How does the Church close the Lord's Prayer?

The Church closes the Lord's Prayer and, in fact, all of her prayers, with "Amen," which expresses her desire that "let it be done to me as you say" (Lk. 1:38), that is, her complete abandonment to the will of the Father.

Appendices

Section I:
History of the Catechism

When was the Catechism of the Catholic Church issued?

The working French-language text of Catechism of the Catholic Church was approved by Pope John Paul II on June 25, 1992, and ordered to be published by the Holy Father in his Apostolic Constitution *Fidei Depositum* of October 11, 1992. Since then, the Catechism has been published in virtually all major modern languages. On September 8, 1997, Pope John Paul presented the *editio typica* in Latin.

Why was the Catechism of the Catholic Church issued?

The Extraordinary Synod of Bishops, which met in 1985 to commemorate the twentieth anniversary of the close of the Second Vatican Ecumenical Council, requested in its final report that the Holy Father issue "a catechism or compendium of all Catholic doctrine, covering both faith and morals, which would serve as the a reference text for the catechisms or compendiums which are published in the various different countries." The Extraordinary Synod also requested that the catechism's exposition of doctrine "be both biblical and liturgical, presenting both sure doctrine while at the same time adapted to contemporary Christian life."

What is the doctrinal value of the text of the Catechism of the Catholic Church?

The Holy Father himself, in the Apostolic Constitution *Fidei Depositum*, specified that "this Catechism is given to serve as a sure and authentic reference text for the teaching of Catholic doctrine and especially for the composition of local catechisms." He further noted that the

Catechism is directly related to the office of Peter in the Church since the "approval and publication of the Catechism of the Catholic Church constitutes a service which the successor of Peter renders to the Holy Catholic Church and to all the particular churches in communion with the Apostolic See of Rome: that of sustaining and confirming the faith of all the disciples of the Lord Jesus, and thus, reinforcing the bonds of unity in the same apostolic faith."

To whom is the Catechism of the Catholic Church addressed?

The Catechism is addressed to the pastors of the Church as an aid in their mission of announcing the Gospel to all men. However, it is also addressed to faithful as well as to all men of good will who may "demand the reason of this hope" (1 Pt. 3:15) which the Church has in her Lord who solemnly declared: "I am the light of the world. No follower of mine shall ever walk in darkness; no, he shall possess the light of life" (Jn 8:12).

Section II:
The Seven Sacraments:
A Summary

BAPTISM

Minister:
- Bishop
- Priest
- Deacon
- (In case of emergency, anyone with the intention of doing what the Church does)

Recipient:
- Any unbaptized person

Essential Rite:
- Pouring of or immersion in water with the words: *(Name), I baptize you in the name of the Father and of the Son and of the Holy Spirit.*

Effects:
- Baptism cleanses the soul of sin, original and personal, and makes one a child of God, incorporated into the Church. It also bestows the gifts of the Holy Spirit, giving the baptized a share in God's life (sanctifying grace), and in faith, hope, and chariy. Baptism indelibly marks the soul.

CONFIRMATION

Minister:
- Bishop
- Priest (by delegation)

Recipient:
- In the Roman Rite, any baptized person who is of the age of reason and not yet confirmed. In the Eastern Rites any baptized person is eligible.

Essential Rite:
- Laying on of hands and annointing with the sacred Chrism with the words: *(Name), be sealed with the gift of the Holy Spirit.*

Effects:
- Confirmation indelibly marks the soul, sealing and strengthening the baptismal call to be conformed to Christ as priest, prophet, and king. It empowers those confirmed in the Holy Spirit to witness to their faith.

EUCHARIST

Minister:
- Bishop
- Priest

Recipient:
- Baptized persons who are properly disposed, that is, who believe in the Real Presence and are in a state of grace

Essential Rite:
- Changing the bread and the wine into the Body and Blood of Christ by the words: *This is my body, which will be given up for you. . . . This is the cup of my blood, the blood of the new and everlasting covenant. It will be shed for you and for all so that sins may be forgiven. Do this in memory of me.*

Effects:
- The Eucharist nourishes the life of grace by deepening the recipient's union with Christ and, through him, with the Father and the Holy Spirit, as well as with all members of his Body. It also obtains the forgiveness of venial sins.

PENANCE

Minister:
- Bishop
- Priest

Recipient:
- Any baptized person who has committed sin and is sincerely sorry for having offended God by sin

Essential Rite:
- Contrition for and confession of sins, penance, and the words of absolution: *God the Father of mercies, through the death and resurrection of his Son has reconciled the world to himself and sent the Holy Spirit among us for the forgiveness of sins; through the ministry of the Church, may God give you pardon and peace, and **I absolve you from your sins in the name of the Father, and of the Son, and of the Holy Spirit.***

Effects:
- Penance effects the forgiveness of sins, reconciliation with God and the community, and an increase in grace and the virtue of charity.

ANOINTING OF THE SICK

Minister: • Bishop
                   • Priest

Recipient: • Any baptized person who is infirm or elderly or in danger of death

Essential Rite: • Anointing of the recipient's forehead with holy oil with the words: *Through this holy annointing, may the Lord in his love and mercy help you with the grace of the Holy Spirit;* then anointing of the recipient's hands with holy oil with the words: *May the Lord who frees you from sin save you and raise you up.*

Effects: • Anointing of the sick unites the recipient with the passion of Christ, for the sick person's own good and that of the whole Church and at the same time grants strength, peace, and courage to endure as a Christian the sufferings of illness or old age. The sacrament also brings forgiveness of sins, if the sick person was not able to obtain it through the sacrament of Penance, restoration of health, if it is conducive to the salvation of the soul, and prepares the recipient to enter into eternal life.

HOLY ORDERS

Minister: • Bishop

Recipient: • Any man who, having completed Christian initiation (Baptism, Confirmation, Eucharist) and meeting the prerequisites of this sacrament, is accepted as a candidate for ordination by the Church

Essential Rite: • Laying on of hands and the words of the consecratory prayer proper to each order

Effects: • The sacrament increases grace, indelibly marking the soul of the person receiving the sacrament and conferring the special power of the order (diaconate, priesthood, or episcopate) received.

MATRIMONY

Minister:
- Bride and groom (the bishop, priest, or deacon witnesses the sacrament in the name of the Church)

Recipient:
- Any baptized man or woman who is free to marry and willingly enters into a lifelong matrimonial covenant

Essential Rite:
- The marriage covenant is effected by the bride and groom consenting to give themselves permanently to each other in the presence of the Church and her witness.

Effects:
- The marriage covenant increases grace and, in uniting the husband and wife indissolubly to each other in Christ and making of them a sign of God's spousal covenant with the Church, also gives them special graces to enable them to fulfill the obligations they assume.

Section III:
Church Laws Concerning Marriage*

Matrimony—defined as the *marriage covenant by which a man and woman establish between themselves a partnership of the whole of life—is by its nature ordered towards the good of the spouses and the procreation and education of offspring.* For a baptized couple, this covenant has been raised by Christ to the dignity of a sacrament. Because Christ instituted this sacrament, he also gives a man and a woman their vocation to marriage. The covenant thus involves not only a man and a woman, but also Christ. In establishing marriage as a vocation in life, God gave it the characteristics that enable human love to achieve its perfection and allow family life to be full and fruitful. Outside marriage, or without a proper realization of its nature, the right conditions for the fruitfulness of human love and for a successful family life do not exist.

The Catholic Church has the right to establish laws regarding the validity of marriages, since marriage for the baptized is both a covenant and a sacrament. And it is only the Catholic Church that has jurisdiction over those marriages, with due regard for the competence of civil authority concerning the merely civil effects. No one other than the Church has the power or authority to change ecclesiastical laws.

UNITY AND INDISSOLUBILITY

Unity of marriage signifies that the *covenant* established is between one man and one woman: the husband cannot marry another woman during the lifetime of his wife, nor can the wife marry another man during the lifetime of her husband. *Polygamy*—having more than one spouse at the same time—is contrary to the equal personal dignity of men and women, who in Matrimony give themselves with a love that is total and, therefore unique and exclusive.

Indissolubility refers to the fact that the bond of sacramental marriage cannot be broken except by the death of either the husband or the wife.

* Taken from the *Handbook of Prayers* by James Socías, published by Midwest Theological Forum, Chicago and Scepter Publications, Princeton, New Jersey. With permission.

CONSENT

Matrimonial consent is an act of the will by which a man and a woman, in an irrevocable covenant, mutually give and accept each other, declaring their willingness to welcome children and to educate them. Consent must be a free act of the will of each of the contracting parties, without coercion or serious fear arising from external circumstances. To be free means:

- *To be acting without constraint.*
- *To be unimpeded by natural or ecclesiastical law.*

Only those capable of giving valid matrimonial consent can get married: Matrimony is created through the consent of the parties—consent legitimately manifested between persons who, according to law, are capable of giving that consent.

CONDITIONS FOR A VALID MARRIAGE

1. The contracting parties must be capable, according to Church law, of giving matrimonial consent. Before Matrimony is celebrated, it must be evident that no impediment stands in the way of its valid and licit (lawful) celebration.
2. The consent given by the parties must be deliberate, fully voluntary, free, mutual, and public. Therefore, the following are incapable of contracting marriage:
   - Persons who lack sufficient use of reason.
   - Persons who suffer from grave lack of discretion of judgment concerning essential matrimonial rights and duties that are to be mutually given and accepted.
   - Persons who, because of serious psychic illness, cannot assume the essential obligations of Matrimony.
3. The consent must be *legitimately manifested in canonical form*, in the presence of an authorized priest or deacon and two witnesses. Canonical form does not oblige non-Catholics when they marry other non-Catholics, but only Catholics—even if only one of the two parties is Catholic—who have not left the Church by a formal act. *The priest or deacon who assists at the celebration of a marriage receives the consent of the spouses in the name of the Church and gives them the blessing of the Church. The presence of the Church's minister, as well as that of the witnesses, visibly expresses the fact that marriage is an ecclesial reality.*

AGE REQUIREMENT

As a condition for marriage, the Church requires that a man has completed his sixteenth year (one's sixteenth year is completed the day after one's sixteenth birthday) and that a woman has completed her fourteenth year of age (one's fourteenth year of age is completed the day after one's fourteenth birthday). These ages are the minima for validity. There may be civil laws, as well, regulating the minimum age for each state and country, but failure to comply with these laws does not invalidate marriage in the eyes of the Church.

INVALID MARRIAGES

Marriage is permanent, because God established it so from the very beginning. The indissolubility of marriage is for the good of husband and wife, their children, and human society as a whole. The civil government has no power to dissolve a valid marriage—even if the marriage is between non-Catholics.

The government can dissolve only the civil aspects of marriage, such as ownership of property, custody of the children, etc. *Even when civil divorce is allowed by the country's law*, marriage, in God's eyes, still exists.

The Church does not have the power to dissolve a valid, sacramental marriage that has been *consummated*. She may declare a marriage *null and void* only upon investigation and on evidence that the marriage did not exist from the very beginning. The reasons could be one of the following:

- Lack of fully *voluntary and free consent*.
- Some deficiency in the *form of the marriage celebration*.
- The presence of an *impediment* that makes a marriage invalid.

The *declaration of nullity* (so-called *annulment*) is a very important decision of an ecclesiastical court. A careful investigation has to be made by the court before that conclusion can be reached, ensuring that no valid marriage is declared *null and void* by mistake.

MIXED MARRIAGES

Marriages between a Catholic and a baptized Christian who is not in full communion with the Catholic Church are called *mixed marriages*. For *mixed marriages*, permission (not dispensation) from the local ordinary (usually the bishop) is required for validity. Marriages between Catholics and unbaptized persons (*disparity of cult*) are invalid unless a dispensation from the local ordinary is granted. All this presupposes that these marriages are celebrated with all other necessary conditions fulfilled.

The local bishop may grant permission or dispensation for such marriages on the following conditions:

- The Catholic party declares that he or she is prepared to remove dangers of falling away from the faith and makes a sincere promise to do all in his or her power to have all the children baptized and brought up in the Catholic Church.

- The other party is to be informed at an appropriate time of these promises that the Catholic person has to make. It is important that the other person be truly aware of the commitments and obligations of the Catholic spouse.
- Both persons are to be instructed with respect to the essential ends and properties of marriage, which are not to be excluded by either party.
- The man and woman should *marry in the Catholic Church*. The canonical form (Church ceremony with an authorized Catholic priest or deacon and at least two other witnesses present) is to be followed. When there are serious difficulties, the local bishop may give a dispensation and allow another form which is public (such as a civil ceremony) to be followed. It is never allowed, however, to have the Catholic priest or deacon and a non-Catholic minister, rabbi, or public official, each performing his or her own rite, asking for the consent of the parties. Likewise, it is forbidden to have another religious marriage ceremony before or after the Catholic ceremony for giving or receiving the matrimonial consent. Marriage consent is given only once.

WORTHY RECEPTION OF THE SACRAMENT

Once these requirements for a valid marriage are fulfilled, some other conditions are needed for the *worthy* reception of the *sacrament* of Matrimony:

- *Baptism.* Both parties must be baptized persons.
- *Rectitude of intention.* Being carried away by emotions or momentary passions should be avoided. Premarital pregnancy is not a sufficient reason to marry someone, as that could involve an added mistake.
- *Spiritual preparation.* One should be in the state of grace. The sacraments of Penance and holy Eucharist are strongly recommended as immediate preparation.
- *Confirmation.* Catholics should have previously received the sacrament of Confirmation. This sacrament should be received before marriage, unless grave difficulties stand in the way.
- *Knowledge of the duties of married life.* Such duties include mutual fidelity of the spouses until death, and care for the bodily and spiritual welfare of the children sent by God.
- *Obedience to the marriage laws of the Church.*

Section IV:
Basic Prayers*

SIGN OF THE CROSS

By the sign of the cross deliver us from our enemies, you who are our God.

In the name of the Father, and of the Son, and of the Holy Spirit. Amen.

LORD'S PRAYER

Our Father, who art in heaven, hallowed be thy name. Thy kingdom come; thy will be done on earth as it is in heaven. Give us this day our daily bread; and forgive us our trespasses as we forgive those who trespass against us; and lead us not into temptation, but deliver us from evil. Amen.

HAIL MARY

Hail, Mary, full of grace, the Lord is with thee; blessed art thou among women, and blessed is the fruit of thy womb Jesus. Holy Mary, Mother of God, pray for us sinners, now and at the hour of our death. Amen.

GLORY BE

Glory be to the Father, and to the Son, and to the Holy Spirit. As it was in the beginning, is now, and ever shall be, world without end. Amen.

SPIRITUAL COMMUNION

I wish, my Lord, to receive you with the purity, humility and devotion with which your most holy Mother received you, with the spirit and fervor of the saints.

---

* Taken from the *Handbook of Prayers* by James Socías, published by Midwest Theological Forum, Chicago and Scepter Publications, Princeton, New Jersey. With permission.

ACT OF FAITH

O my God, I firmly believe that you are one God in three divine Persons, Father, Son and Holy Spirit; I believe that your divine Son became man and died for our sins, and that he shall come to judge the living and the dead. I believe these and all the truths that the holy Catholic Church teaches, because you have revealed them, who can neither deceive nor be deceived.

ACT OF HOPE

O my God, relying on your almighty power and infinite mercy and promises, I hope to obtain pardon for my sins, the help of your grace, and life everlasting, through the merits of Jesus Christ, my Lord and Redeemer.

ACT OF CHARITY

O my God, I love you above all things, with my whole heart and soul, because you are all-good and worthy of all love. I love my neighbor as myself for the love of you. I forgive all who have injured me and ask pardon of all whom I have injured.

ACT OF CONTRITION

O my God, I am heartily sorry for having offended you, and I detest all my sins, because I dread the loss of heaven and the pains of hell; but most of all because they offend you, my God, who are all good and deserving of all my love. I firmly resolve, with the help of your grace, to confess my sins, to do penance, and to amend my life. Amen.

PRAYER TO THE HOLY SPIRIT
(Blessed Josemaría Escrivá)

Come, O Holy Spirit! Enlighten my understanding in order that I may know your commands; strengthen my heart against the snares of the enemy; enkindle my will. I have heard your voice, and I do not want to harden my heart and resist, saying, "Later . . . tomorrow." *Nunc coepi!* Right now! Lest there be no tomorrow for me.

O Spirit of truth and of wisdom, Spirit of understanding and of counsel, Spirit of joy and of peace! I want what you want, because you want it, as you want it, when you want it.

APOSTLES' CREED

I believe in God, the Father almighty, Creator of heaven and earth. I believe in Jesus Christ, his only Son, Our Lord. He was conceived by the power of the Holy Spirit and born of the Virgin Mary. He suffered under Pontius Pilate, was crucified, died, and was buried. He descended to the dead. On the third day he rose again. He ascended into heaven, and is seated the right hand of the Father. He will come again to judge the living and the dead. I believe in the Holy Spirit, the holy Catholic Church, the communion of saints, the forgiveness of sins, the resurrection of the body, and the life everlasting. Amen.

NICENE-CONSTANTINOPOLITAN CREED

We believe in one God, the Father, the Almighty, maker of heaven and earth, of all that is seen and unseen. We believe in one Lord, Jesus Christ, the only Son of God, eternally begotten of the Father, God from God, Light from Light, true God from true God, begotten, not made, one in Being with the Father. Through him all things were made. For us men and for our salvation he came down from heaven: by the power of the Holy Spirit he was born of the Virgin Mary, and became man. For our sake he was crucified under Pontius Pilate; he suffered, died, and was buried. On the third day he rose again in fulfillment of the Scriptures; he ascended into heaven and is seated at the right hand of the Father. He will come again in glory to judge the living and the dead, and his kingdom will have no end. We believe in the Holy Spirit, the Lord, the giver of life, who proceeds from the Father and the Son. With the Father and the Son he is worshiped and glorified. He has spoken through the prophets. We believe in one holy catholic and apostolic Church. We acknowledge one baptism for the forgiveness of sins. We look for the resurrection of the dead, and the life of the world to come. Amen.

PRAYER TO ONE'S GUARDIAN ANGEL

Angel of God, my guardian dear, to whom his love commits me here, ever this day (or night) be at my side, to light and guard, to rule and guide. Amen.

PRAYER TO OUR REDEEMER

Soul of Christ, sanctify me.
Body of Christ, heal me.
Blood of Christ, drench me.
Water from the side of Christ, wash me.
Passion of Christ, strengthen me.
Good Jesus, hear me.
In your wounds shelter me.
From turning away keep me.
From the evil one protect me.
At the hour of my death call me.
Into your presence lead me,
to praise you with all your saints
for ever and ever. Amen.

PRAYING THE ROSARY

The Rosary is divided into three parts; each part, into five mysteries. For each mystery one Our Father and ten Hail Marys (a "decade") are said. In many Christian families, there is a pious custom of reciting daily a third part of the Rosary.

Each decade is a contemplation of the life of our Lord, witnessed by Mary—one aspect of the paschal mystery. At the end of the Rosary you may say the Hail Holy Queen.

Joyful Mysteries

(Mondays, Thursdays and Sundays of Advent)

1. The Annunciation
2. The Visitation
3. The Nativity
4. The Presentation
5. The Finding of Jesus in the Temple

Sorrowful Mysteries

(Tuesdays, Fridays and Sundays of Lent)

1. The Agony in the Garden
2. The Scourging at the Pillar
3. The Crowning with Thorns
4. The Carrying of the Cross
5. The Crucifixion

Glorious Mysteries

(Wednesdays, Saturdays and Sundays from Easter until Advent)

1. The Resurrection
2. The Ascension
3. The Descent of the Holy Spirit
4. The Assumption
5. The Coronation of the BlessedVirgin Mary

HAIL HOLY QUEEN

Hail, holy Queen, mother of mercy, our life, our sweetness, and our hope. To you do we cry, poor banished children of Eve. To you do we send up our sighs, mourning and weeping in this valley of tears. Turn then, most gracious advocate, your eyes of mercy toward us, and after this exile show us the blessed fruit of your womb, Jesus. O clement, O loving, O sweet Virgin Mary. Pray for us, O Holy Mother of God. That we may be made worthy of the promises of Christ.

THE MEMORARE
(St. Bernard)

Remember, O most gracious Virgin Mary, that never was it known that anyone who fled to your protection, implored your help or sought your intercession, was left unaided. Inspired by this confidence, I fly unto you, O Virgin of virgins, my Mother. To you I come, before you I stand, sinful and sorrowful. O Mother of the Word Incarnate, despise not my petitions, but, in your mercy, hear and answer me. Amen.

ANGELUS

V. The angel of the Lord declared unto Mary;
R. **And she conceived of the Holy Spirit.**
Hail Mary . . .
V. Behold the handmaid of the Lord.
R. **Be it done unto me according to your word.**
Hail Mary . . .
V. And the Word was made flesh.
R. **And dwelt among us.**
Hail Mary . . .
V. Pray for us, O holy Mother of God.
R. **That we may be made worthy of the promises of Christ.**

Pour forth, we beseech you, O Lord, your grace into our hearts, that we to whom the incarnation of Christ, your Son, was made known by the message of an angel, may by his passion and cross be brought to the glory of his resurrection, through the same Christ our Lord.

R. Amen.

REGINA CÆLI
(Easter Time)

V. Queen of heaven, rejoice! Alleluia.
R. **For he whom you did merit to bear. Alleluia.**
V. Has risen, as he said. Alleluia.
R. **Pray for us to God. Alleluia.**
V. Rejoice and be glad, O Virgin Mary. Alleluia.
R. **For the Lord is truly risen. Alleluia.**

O God, who gave joy to the world through the resurrection of your Son our Lord Jesus Christ, grant, we beseech you, that through the intercession of the Virgin Mary, his Mother, we may obtain the joys of everlasting life, through the same Christ our Lord.

R. Amen.

Index

Index *

---

* The numerical references in the index refer to the appropriate questions in this book.

Scandal 166, 171

Scripture 11, 12, 15-18, 22, 178,
    198, 223, 244

Sermons 137, 145

Sick, The 71, 93, 94

Sin 33, 124-128, 149, 155, 158,
    165, 166, 170, 171, 175, 183,
    190, 196, 233, 240-242, 245

Sin, Original 34-36, 43, 44

Sin and Salvation 38, 46, 47

Sin and Sacraments 75, 85-91,
    94

Sin and Indulgences 92

Sin and Justification 138

Sin, Forgiveness of 204, 229, 239

Social Justice 133, 186

Society 54, 101, 129-131, 140,
    141, 162, 163, 187

Society and Duties 162, 163

Society and Marriage 101

Society, Church as a 54

Solidarity 124, 163

Son, God the (Jesus Christ) 9,
    19, 24, 26, 27, 29, 37, 40, 42,
    45-47, 53, 67, 75, 76, 151,
    209, 226, 231, 236, 237, 240

Sorrow 206
    see also Sadness

Soul 48, 53, 62, 67-69, 82, 105,
    142, 146, 185, 213, 228

Struggle, Christian 91, 193, 216

Sundays 143, 157, 158, 211

T

Temperance 113, 117, 193

Temptation 220, 229, 241, 242

Thanksgiving 202, 203, 206

Trinity, Blessed 26, 27, 57, 118,
    129, 209, 227

Truth 2, 9, 10, 16, 23, 24, 26, 30,
    37, 50, 58, 59, 77, 136, 142,
    174, 185, 189, 191, 235

U

Unity 21, 163

Unity of the Church 54, 66, 81,
    101

Unity of Person 176, 177

Unity of the Trinity 26

V

Venial Sin 126

Vigilance 218, 241

Virgin Mary 23, 37, 38, 42, 45,
    67, 69, 155, 200

Virtues 109, 113, 118, 121, 208

Vocation 139, 174, 191, 233

W

War 172

Weaknesses 14, 197

Will of God 46, 77, 236, 237

Woman 101, 161, 174, 176, 178

Work 70, 156-158, 186, 187

Worship 70, 72, 73, 78, 148, 152,
    157